Stephen Higginson Tyng

The Captive Orphan; Esther, the Queen of Persia

Stephen Higginson Tyng

The Captive Orphan; Esther, the Queen of Persia

ISBN/EAN: 9783744660907

Printed in Europe, USA, Canada, Australia, Japan

Cover: Foto ©ninafisch / pixelio.de

More available books at **www.hansebooks.com**

THE

CAPTIVE ORPHAN:

ESTHER,

THE QUEEN OF PERSIA.

BY

STEPHEN H. TYNG, D.D.,

RECTOR OF ST. GEORGE'S CHURCH, NEW YORK.

NEW YORK:
ROBERT CARTER & BROTHERS,
530 BROADWAY.

1860.

Entered, according to Act of Congress, in the year 1859, by
STEPHEN H. TYNG,
In the Clerk's Office of the District Court for the Southern District of New York.

STEREOTYPED BY
T. B. SMITH & SON,
84 Beekman-st., N.Y.

PRINTED BY
E. O. JENKINS
26 Frankfort-st.

TABLE OF CONTENTS.

	PAGE
Introduction,	5
I.—The Captive's Vision,	9
II.—The Symbol of Providence,	25
III.—The Ruler of the Kingdoms,	44
IV.—The Great Lesson,	60
V.—The First Experience,	77
VI.—The Bitter Disappointment,	95
VII.—The Ripened Fruits of Sin,	113
VIII.—The Short-lived Treasure,	134
IX.—The Weak and Lowly,	154
X.—The Beginning of True Prosperity,	171
XI.—The Mysterious Beginning,	189
XII.—The Important Friendship,	207
XIII.—The Guardianship of Grace,	224
XIV.—The Time for Usefulness,	244
XV.—Difficulties Cleared up,	262
XVI.—The Righteous Ruler,	280
XVII.—Vain Prosperity,	299
XVIII.—Plotting in Vain,	317
XIX.—The Wicked Overthrown,	335
XX.—Unexpected Results,	354
XXI.—Tried Fidelity,	373
XXII.—The End in Peace,	392

INTRODUCTION.

Four years since I prepared for the press a course of lectures to the younger members of my beloved flock, on the history of Ruth, under the title of The Rich Kinsman. They have been well received, abundantly circulated, and in many instances made useful. The success of that effort has encouraged me to prepare another similar course on the history of Esther. These were familiarly delivered to the same class of hearers on the afternoons of the Sabbath, and have been written for the press amidst all my pressure of other cares and duties.

The history of Ruth illustrates, in a very distinct and beautiful manner, the great Scripture doctrine of Redemption. The history of Esther, in an equally clear and striking manner, delineates and explains the great doctrine of Divine Providence. It brings out this subject, in a peculiarly dramatic style of exhibition, in a series of living illustrations. The truths which are to be taught utter themselves naturally in the actions and trials of the persons whose history is described. The whole story becomes a constant exhibition of the native purposes of man, and a manifestation as constant, of the power and interposition of God.

Four separate characters, perfectly distinct from each other, and each illustrating perfectly distinct lessons of truth and wisdom for man, are interwoven in a constant connection with each other in the process of the story. They act in a spontaneous demonstration of their own individual feelings and motives, in the various circumstances in which they are placed. They are entirely independent of each other in the separate schemes and purposes which they are led to pursue; and each of them works out, in a consistent and undeviating course, the peculiar principles by which they are separately governed, in a perfectly natural method of exhibition. Yet they are thoroughly combined in the great plot of the history, as agents and instruments of an overruling providence of which they know but little, and of which some of them have not a single thought. Thus the whole story becomes to us who read it, one of the most distinct and beautiful illustrations of the gracious providence of God which any human history could give, and makes the sacred Book which contains it, one of the most interesting and attractive of the Scriptures of the Old Testament.

Under this aspect I have endeavored to present the instructions which it contains, and some of the various truths which arise out of them, for general improvement. How adequately and satisfactorily this has been done, others will necessarily judge. I acknowledge, on the review of the whole, a perception of the partial and superficial manner in which the work has been accomplished ; but, I trust, the whole teaching of the book will be found to be accordant with truth, and adapted to the profit and advantage of the youthful minds for whom it has been prepared. It is a blessed characteristic of the present age of the Church, that so much effort and provision are made for the religious teaching of the young. Every mature mind will feel and acknowledge, that in this there is a most promising commencement at the right end of our great work, and rejoice in the wisdom, as well as in the encouragement and success of the plan which it displays. So much of my own ministry has always been given to the young, and such abundant and blessed fruits of Christian success have been gathered under it from the young, that I welcome from my heart every new faithful laborer in the same happy field, and urge upon my brethren in the ministry everywhere, to follow their Lord's beautiful example in taking the little ones under their tender care, and to rejoice in being made for Him "teachers of babes."

To the many dear youths whom the gracious Saviour has been pleased to place under my own ministry, I affectionately dedicate and offer this new work, beseeching Him to make it a blessing to them all, through the riches of His grace.

S. H. T.

St George's Rectory, *September* 1, 1859.

THE CAPTIVE ORPHAN.

I.

The Captive's Vision.

"The heavens were opened, and I saw the visions of God."—EZEKIEL, i. 1.

THIS was the vision of a captive; not the captive orphan of whom I am to speak, but another earlier captive of the same nation, and in the same region of country. The life of Esther, the Captive Orphan, was a remarkable illustration of the divine Providence, in the story of its facts. And this vision of Ezekiel the earlier captive was an illustration of the same Providence equally remarkable, in the symbols and images which it contains. I may, therefore, with propriety employ the vision of the one captive to introduce the story of the other.

Ezekiel was among the Jewish captives by the river of Chebar. His spirit was depressed and sad. To be a bondman to labor on another's soil, and an exile from the land of his birth and the home of his fathers, was for him a new and a hard life. He had not been educated under the burdens of bodily toil, nor accustomed to the weariness of a life of subjection. His birthright made him a priest in Israel. His family gave him exalted rank among his people. His education had accustomed him to the habits of a refined and contemplative man. And when he was carried away among the captive Israelites to Babylon, this extreme change in his life must have made the burden which it brought upon him still the heavier, and the sorrows which attended his new lot far harder to bear.

In such circumstances the remembrance of the past and the fear of the future would combine their power to distress a refined and sensitive spirit. They would be considered the happiest who had the least to lose, or whose dullness of feeling and hardiness of habit could exclude the secret sorrows of the heart, and diminish the anguish of the bodily pain. But an educated captive, with a high and noble soul that will be free and can not be enslaved, with affections, thoughts and memories that must go out, and can not be still; with many secret questions about the providence which has allowed the trial, that God alone can answer, but which man longs to solve; exhibits, perhaps ,as heavy a burden as man is ever required to bear.

And this was the condition of Ezekiel, the priest of Israel. The beauty of the outward scenery could afford no diversion to his mind. The gratification of the mere needs of the body could furnish no relief. His sorrows were the sorrows of a wounded spirit. Who could bear them? Dumb nature around him was clothed with charms. The willow-fringed rivers of Babylon were beautiful.

"The dirge of nature is her streams!
Their song speaks a soft music to man's grief;
And those must love them, who have loved
All else in vain."

Yet Ezekiel could only join in the sad song of his captive countrymen: "By the rivers of Babylon we sat down. Yea, we wept when we remembered Zion. We hanged our harps upon the willows in the midst thereof. For they that carried us away captive required of us a song. And they that wasted us required of us mirth, saying, Sing us one of the songs of Zion. How shall we sing the Lord's song in a strange land?"

Ezekiel saw a world of beauty there. The overhanging skies of Chaldea were bright and full of instruction. Long had men employed the calm nights and level plains of that lovely land to study and to classify the heavenly scenery. The captive priest was not blind to all this beauty, nor ignorant, nor careless, of the divine glory which was displayed in these wonderful works of God. Often had he sung at home the beautiful words of the sweet singer of Israel—"When I consider thy heavens, the work of thy fingers, the moon and the stars which thou hast ordained; what is man that thou art mindful of him? or the son of man that thou visitest him?" "The heavens declare the glory of God, and the firmament showeth his handiwork." He could have told the wisest star-gazers in Babylon, truths concerning those heavenly worlds which they had never discerned. He could have taught them who it was "that covered himself with light as with a garment," and "stretched out the heavens as a curtain."

But Ezekiel was a captive "among the captives" on the banks of the Chebar. These were not the captive's meditations. They could not divert his sorrows. He thought of his lost home, and of his scattered, suffering people. He "wept in remembrance of Zion." He had seen "Judah gone into captivity, in affliction and great servitude, dwelling among the heathen, and finding no rest." "The Lord had covered the daughter of Zion with a cloud in his anger, and had cast down from the heavens unto the earth the beauty of Israel." And neither the soft-flowing waters of Chebar, nor the verdant plains of Chaldea could refresh the sorrows of a spirit broken like his. His griefs were abiding, and seemed to be unchangable. Often would he ask himself the meaning and the purpose of this great affliction. Is God unmindful of his covenant? Hath God forgotten to be gracious? Will the Lord cast off for ever? Hath God forsaken his people? These were the captive's questions. But what human reason or wisdom could answer them? These were questions about the divine Providence, about the government and will of God himself. And who but God could tell "the thoughts which He was thinking towards his people"—thoughts which He had declared were "thoughts of peace and not of evil, to give them" the assurance of "an expected end?"

But the captive Israelite was not deserted. God did himself reply, and gave him this wonderful book of divine predictions that he might teach them to his people; and this glorious vision with which its revelations were introduced, that he might thus understand his gracious providence, and explain and justify the ways of God in his government and chastisement of his servants. "The heavens were opened, and he saw the vision of God, and the word of the Lord came expressly to him, and the hand of the Lord was upon him." As he beheld these wonders there came out of the north, down the plains of the Euphrates, a whirlwind, a great cloud and a fire of intense brightness, with its flames wreathed together, and folded into each other. Then four living beings came out of the midst of the fire, each of them as if combined of four distinct creatures in a single human form, with feet and with wings on each of their four sides, so that without turning, they could look and move in four different directions. They shone in the fire like burnished brass, and moved about like flashes of lightning. While he was looking at these he saw standing beside each of them a double wheel of immense circumference, made of two wheels, " a wheel in the middle of a wheel," crossing each other ; and when the living beings moved, the wheels moved with them. And when they were lifted up from the earth, the wheels also were lifted up. Ezekiel saw that all the motions of this wonderful vision, whether of the beings or the wheels, were directed by a living spirit which was in them ; " whithersoever the spirit was to go, they went." Their movements were rapid, terrible and complicated. But there was a living spirit which governed them, and an appointed end which they were to secure.

Above all these, he saw, in the heavens, a

glorious throne like a sapphire stone, and on the throne was seated one in "the appearance of a man." "As the appearance of the bow that is in the clouds in the day of rain, so was the appearance of the brightness round about the throne." "This was the appearance of the likeness of the glory of the Lord." And when he saw this glorious manifestation of the Ruler of all, he fell upon his face, and listened to the heavenly voice which gave him the messages he was to deliver to his people, and taught him the truths which were to comfort and instruct himself.

This is a very barren outline of this remarkable vision. Its details you must study in the chapter itself. But this vision I consider an illustration of the gracious providence of God in the rules which govern it. The glory, the power, the intelligence, the skill, the certainty, and the rapidity which distinguish this divine Providence, are all delineated in the different parts of this vision. The Lord Jesus Christ, who is the head over all things for his church, upon whose shoulders is the government over all, is here displayed in the likeness of man upon the throne. His "throne is forever and ever." He knows what his people want and what his creatures will do. He orders and overrules all the events of earth to produce the results which he has designed, and which he has determined to accomplish. By his Holy Spirit he has called and converted to himself those whom he has chosen in love, purchased by his own blood, and thus teaches to love and follow him. By this Spirit he governs and renews them day by day, and will make them ready for the inheritance of his own glory. For their security and happiness, their education on earth, and their preparation for heaven, his glorious providence is made to work continually, secretly, wonderfully—and yet in his own way always surely, to bless them with the unsearchable riches of his grace. "Whithersoever the Spirit goes," there this gracious governing providence goes also. All things are made to work together for good to those who love him.

As in this vision of Ezekiel, the things of this world may sometimes appear to rush like a whirlwind, threatening to destroy. The divine judgments may seem to be like flames of fire wreathed together, successively unfolding their terrible events among men. The purposes of God may appear to be crossing each other in various directions, apparently designed to produce opposite and irreconcilable results. The grandeur of the divine plans in their revolution, may seem, like Ezekiel's wheels, to have a height which is terrible to behold. They may change and reveal themselves as suddenly as the lightning's flash, so that the expectations of man may be overturned in a moment. But all these providences of God are full of meaning and purpose still. They are "full of eyes round about on every side." They can not be disappointed or deceived. The voices which speak in them may be overwhelming to the mind of man, and fill him with terror and alarm. But there is a voice above them which commands them when and where to go. The gracious Saviour rules them and rules by them all, for a constant blessing upon his chosen people. He governs every part and every operation of them, as the wonderful Counsellor and the everlasting Father of all who love him.

This was the instruction which he gave to Ezekiel in "this vision of God." The particular subject which oppressed the captive's mind was the bondage and the apparent ruin of his own nation. The divine instruction which he received concerning this, fills up the whole book which he was directed to write, and reaches forward through all the depressions of Israel to the final and eternal glory which they are hereafter to receive with Jesus their Messiah, as the people of God. My object in considering this vision is to mark the general principles governing the divine Providence, as an appropriate introduction to our study of that providence in the history of Esther, the captive orphan, of whom we are to speak.

The captive priest was taught that God's providence must explain itself. He could know nothing of it but by divine teaching. In the midst of his sorrowful meditations among his countrymen, the heavens were suddenly opened above him, and a new direction was immediately given to all his thoughts. He was made to look up and wait upon God. Said the dying Dr. Payson to

one of his friends, " Do you know why it is
that I am thus confined upon my back? It is
that I may be made to look upwards." How
hard it is to learn this lesson. We easily look
around us in watchfulness and suspicion. We
easily look back in regret and sorrowful remembrance. We easily look forward in fear, apprehension and unbelief. We easily look within in
despondency, depression, perhaps in self-condemnation and despair. But how hard it is to look
up, with an affectionate acknowledgment of
God, and an expectation from him, with a calm
and filial faith, believing that he doeth all
things well, that there is no evil in the earth,
and the Lord hath not done it. We easily look
around upon the creatures, the possible instruments of our advantage or our sorrow, and either
accuse them in the bitterness of a wounded spirit
as the origin of our sufferings, or call upon them
for a help in our distress which they have no
power to give. But how hard it is to look up to
God in trust and prayer, asking his divine teaching, trusting that as he hath torn, so he will

heal us, as he hath smitten us, so he will bind us up.

Accordingly this is the first lesson we have to learn, that he alone can teach us what his providence means, and our eyes and our hearts must wait upon him. Often does a serious suffering mind, under the darkness of a trial for which it has yet no interpretation, say with Job, "Oh that I knew where I might find him! That I might come even to his seat! Behold I go forward but he is not there; and backward, but I can not perceive him: on the left hand where he doth work, but I can not behold him; he hideth himself on the right hand that I can not see him." Yet Job was taught afterwards to say, with a confidence full of hope, "He knoweth the way that I take, and when he hath tried me I shall come forth as gold;" and with a heart full of self-abasement, "I have heard of thee by the hearing of the ear, but now mine eye seeth thee, wherefore I abhor myself, and repent in dust and ashes."

How often are we like Ezekiel sitting in sadness among his fellow-captives, or like Jacob in his solitary tent at Mamre, ready to say, "All these things are against me." We can not comprehend the dealings of God with us. We need a divine Teacher, as well as a divine Helper. The book of Providence lies open before us, and we are asked, "Understandest thou what thou readest?" and our grieved and burdened hearts reply, "How can I, except some one shall guide me?" Oh, then, let us look up, and lift up our eyes, and seek the offered guidance. We shall not be forsaken. There is one to guide us safely there. The heavens are opened to us. We may see the visions of God. We may see Jesus the Son of man sitting on the throne of power, ordering all things for his chosen people, making them joyful in his love, and ruling the world in righteousness for their welfare. We need only a simple faith in the divine word and promise to see all the truth that Ezekiel saw, and to receive all the instruction that he received. That which God taught the captive prophet by an immediate revelation, he teaches us in that holy word which is the key to all his works.

In this sacred word God has as plainly revealed himself to us as if the heavens were opened in our sight; and he has sent us his own blessed Spirit to show us how to understand and employ this heavenly word, and to make us grateful and submissive under its gracious teachings. There we may have " visions of God," as our Father, our Redeemer, our Comforter, our portion for ever. Nothing is concealed from us, there, that we can understand. Nothing remains a mystery that we need to know. The wisdom of God in his government, the love of God for his people, the faithfulness of God in caring for those who love him, the grace of God in pardoning and saving those who trust in him, the power of God in protecting them, and the glory of God in sanctifying and honoring them, are there all made clear to our view. And as we see these " visions of God," we are ready to cry out, " Happy is that people whose God is the Lord."

There is great light in this holy word of God. When we learn to study it with a true heart and under the Lord's own teaching, every thing is wonderful, more wonderful than ever before. But every thing is clear, attractive and glorious. There we learn what God is doing with us now, and what he means to do with us hereafter. All his ways become plain, because we are taught of God, and have received a submissive and willing spirit from his gift. "The word of the Lord comes expressly to us." The Spirit of life has opened our eyes to read it; has given new life to our hearts in reading it. All is now light in the dealings of God with us, because all is now love in our hearts towards God. He makes us trust in his wisdom, power and truth, and like the captive prophet we fall humbly on our face, and listen to his voice while he speaks in tenderness and mercy to our souls. The glory of the Lord shines brightly and attractively before us, because we are taught to see it shining in the face of Jesus Christ.

II.

The Symbol of Providence.

"A wheel in the middle of a wheel."—EZEKIEL, i. 16.

ALL interpretation of the providence of God must come from God's own teaching concerning it. This was Ezekiel's first lesson in the wonderful vision which he received. But a second lesson as important as this was, that all these providences of God really proceed immediately from himself. When this glorious light appeared from the open heavens, Ezekiel saw a whirlwind coming out of the north. The whirlwind was already a familiar type of the divine judgments to the prophet's mind. David, Isaiah, Jeremiah, in many places, had proclaimed the judgments of God under this expressive figure (Psalm lviii. 9; Isaiah, lxvi. 15; Jeremiah, xxiii. 19;) and the application of the type the prophet had already seen.

The destruction of Jerusalem by the king of

Babylon had come upon them like a whirlwind out of the north. And the conquest of Babylon by the Medes and Persians was also to come like a whirlwind out of the north, suddenly, secretly, irresistibly. They were both divine judgments, coming directly from the Lord himself, and sent by him upon a wicked people. Ezekiel had mourned over the sorrows of his people, under the one judgment, and he was to proclaim the liberty, the return, and the triumph of Israel, to be accomplished by the other. As he thought of the griefs of the past, the Lord taught him to remember that they came from him. A whirlwind from the Lord had brought them. When he asked for the end to which they should be ordered, the Lord taught him that another whirlwind of the Lord, out of the north, should overturn the bondage of his people, and finish the captivity which they endured.

This is a most important lesson to be learned—All from God. Your troubles, difficulties, losses, trials, whatever they may be, and whatever may be the instruments of them, are all from God. This is the teaching of his Word. Your times are in his hands. Your ways are ordered by him. Your breath depends upon his will. All your sorrows and all your joys are parts of his one great plan of education for you to make you meet to be his own for ever. Try to learn this great lesson at once. Never stop short of this all-important truth. Remember who it is that "hath his way in the whirlwind and in the storm," "while the clouds are the dust of his feet." If whirlwinds of distress and anguish appear to be coming upon you, lift up your eyes to your gracious Lord, and realize the precious fact that they come only and always from him. Blessed will you be in the clear perception and acknowledgment of this great lesson of his Word.

Another important truth which the captive now learned was, that these divine providences would explain themselves as they proceeded in their appointed way—

"His purposes will ripen fast,
Unfolding every hour."

So the captive prophet saw it in his vision. He beheld "a great cloud, and a fire infolding itself" with brightness like the color of amber. It appeared a mass of light in the sky, like flames of fire wreathed together. As it approached him, it unrolled itself, and sent off one portion after another of its flames in these successive openings, until there was nothing left before the prophet but a clear and perfect light like transparent amber. The cloud had gone, the flames of fire had also passed away, and the sky before him was perfectly and gloriously bright and clear.

Thus succeeding events explain the providence and purposes of God. We learn what he intended to do, by what he has done. Our Lord said to his disciples, "what I do, ye know not now, but ye shall know hereafter." This testimony is constantly illustrated.

How dark and heavy was the cloud which came over the patriarch Jacob! First, his beloved Joseph was taken away. Then famine came upon his household. Then Simeon was held in distant bondage. Then Benjamin must also go. The old man groaned aloud: "I am bereaved; ye will bring my gray hairs down with sorrow to the grave. All these things are against me." The flames of fire were wreathed together, infolding themselves. He could distinguish nothing. But how rapidly the cloud unfolded itself! Step by step the purposes of God came out to view. And when at last he beheld his darling Joseph on the throne of Egypt, and embraced in his arms his long-lost son, and saw the children of this beloved son come to him for the patriarch's blessing from God, then all the infolding of the cloud was gone, and the light shone around him as clear as amber. With what gladness did he exclaim, "I did not think to see thy face, and lo, God hath showed me also thy seed."

How dark and heavy was the cloud which came upon Joseph himself! First he was awakened in his youth by mysterious dreams. Then his brethren hated him. They cast him into a pit to die. They sold him as a slave to a caravan of traders. Again he was sold to an Egyptian governor. He was thrown into fearful temptations to sin. He was cast into prison, as the recompense of his fidelity and virtue. There he was forgotten by those whom he had favored. Thirteen years of darkness and suspense passed, while all the flames were infolded, wreathed together, and nothing hopeful or encouraging could be discovered. But when the famine came, and Pharaoh placed him on the throne, and his brethren appeared before him to ask for bread, how rapidly the cloud began to unfold itself. And when he found himself the appointed preserver for his own dear father, and once more permitted to clasp in his arms that loved and venerated form; when all his father's family were in Egypt, gathered under his protection and fed by his hands, the cloud was completely scattered, and the surrounding light was clear as amber. "Be not grieved nor angry with yourselves," he said to his brethren, "that ye sold me hither, for God did send me before you to preserve life; so now it was not you that sent me hither, but God."

My dear young friends, it will be always so, in the divine Providence over the people of

God. If we study the Lord's providence, remembering that all its events come from God, and that God alone can teach us what is their meaning and design; if we wait upon God with patient faith in his divine teaching, to see what he means to do with us, all the flames will unfold themselves in due time. The whirlwind will pass by. The clouds will scatter, and light alone, the purest light, will remain to shine around us, "clear as amber."

Another lesson which the captive prophet learned was, that all the providences of God have a fixed purpose, and are wisely arranged in their operation. There is no blind chance in the government of God, or in the affairs of men. These providences may not be perfectly explicable to us at the time of their occurrence; but we may be sure that God is ruling in them, according to his own plan of wisdom and goodness, and he will certainly bring out from them the results which he has appointed. This important lesson Ezekiel learned in his vision. The whirlwind and the cloud came with their accustomed vehemence. The fire rushed on, unfolded itself, and passed by. Then the four living creatures came forth out of the midst of the fire, as illustrations of the great truths which God was now about to teach his servant. These wonderful beings were the very types of intelligence. They had faces looking at once in four different directions. These faces were symbols of reason, of watchfulness, of steadiness, of power, in the figures of a man, of an eagle, of an ox and of a lion. They had wings for motion in every different direction. Under their wings were the hands of a man, the index of dexterity and skill, for the accomplishment of their appointed ends. And their whole appearance was like burning coals of fire, and sparkled like the color of burnished brass. We could hardly imagine all the constituents of great intelligence combined in a more remarkable manner than this. These wonderful beings were emblems of the skill, intelligence and wisdom which govern the providences of God.

When one asked Dr. Payson if he could discern any reason for his great personal sufferings, he answered, "No; but I am as well satisfied

THE SYMBOL OF PROVIDENCE.

as if I saw ten thousand reasons. The will of God is the perfection of all reason." The ways and thoughts of God are not like ours. He does not give to us a previous account of his plans and purposes. But he knows the thoughts which he thinks concerning us. And he makes us to see and acknowledge at last, how wise and how perfect they all were. Thus every providence appears to us with the face of a man, open, intelligent and clear, having a manifest design, and perfectly adapted to accomplish it. It has also the eye of an eagle, which seeth afar off. It is watchful over the least of the affairs which it includes. The very hairs of our head, the stones in our path, the moments of our unconscious sleep, are all the subjects of its provision and control. These providences are also perfectly steady and uniform in their operation. The Lord is of one mind and changeth not; the same yesterday, to-day and for ever. Their steadiness of aspect and motion is like the face of an ox, patient, constant, pressing on, slowly perhaps, but surely, in its appointed path, for the attainment of its expected end. They are also the agents of resistless power. They have a face like a lion. God works according to his own will. None can resist, and none are allowed to ask, "What doest thou?" In his hand we are as clay in the hands of the potter; and our security and peace are to be found in our quietness and submission to his will. The skill and adaptation of these providences are also equally remarkable. The hands of a man are under their wings, showing that all the wonderful elements which have been seen before, are wisely and skillfully directed, and will accurately accomplish their fixed design.

All these elements of intelligence, wisdom and power become plain to us as the providences of God are gradually unfolded to our view. The whole plan, at first, may be so wreathed together that it is indistinct and unintelligible to us. It comes over us like a cloud or a whirlwind. Its judgments often seem to us fiery and fearful. But let us wait. Soon the flames will unfold themselves. Light will break forth from the midst of them; living agents of wisdom and power become revealed; and as the work goes on, we see at last that "the work of the Lord is perfect;" and that infinite wisdom and skill have arranged and guided the whole. Then we rejoice in the light of the Lord, and are ready to exclaim with gratitude, "He doeth all things well."

Again, the prophet was taught that the same providences are often designed to produce separate and sometimes apparently opposite results. We can never affirm that all the Lord's plans of wisdom and mercy in any particular dispensation have been completed. The captive prophet saw these living beings moving in every direction with equal ease. They were ready to go with their wings or with their wheels, with the utmost rapidity, in whatever course they were directed, for the fulfillment of their Ruler's will. They "ran and returned as the appearance of a flash of lightning;" suddenly changing their course, rushing forward in a new direction, and for the attainment of an unexpected end. There was also a "wheel in the middle of a wheel" moving as readily in one direction as in another. "They turned not when they went."

This is a frequent exhibition of the providences of God. While they seem to be accomplishing one design, there is another purpose also found to be attained, which was not suspected. Persons, things, and interests, which we had not taken into consideration as any part of the scheme of operation, are discovered, as they proceed, to be not only a part, but often, apparently, a large part of their original design.

These various results of Providence, and the instruments by which they are completed, are not generally wonderful or strange things. They are perfectly natural and common things, but brought about by ways which we had not anticipated. They are things which occur just as naturally as a wheel revolves, or as wings support in flight. But they come and go in their particular occurrence as God directs, and they bring to pass the designs which God has formed. What was more natural in the case of the infant Moses, when he was exposed upon the Nile, than that a loving sister should follow and watch the course of his little ark? What could be more natural than that Pharaoh's daughter and her maidens should come down there to bathe? But how wise and intelligent was the providence which brought these different things together, that Moses might be nursed and educated, and qualified for the great work which God had assigned to him in his future life, as the deliverer of his people! How great was the result which here depended on the motion of the wheel in the middle of the wheel! And how rapid was the change in the whole scheme of motion, which perhaps in an hour converted a poor outcast babe, doomed to apparent death, to a child of royalty, to be prepared for exaltation and honor.

The captivity of the Jews in Babylon was designed to punish their rebellion against the Lord their God. But it was also designed to sanctify and preserve the real people of God from whom the Saviour was to come, and to prepare the way for his appearing. Babylon was to be taken and overthrown with great violence for the wickedness of the people of that kingdom. But it was also to give way to another, and another kingdom, till he should come, who was to be the great Ruler over all for ever. Thus Ezekiel was taught. He saw these wonderful beings rushing like the lightning, first one way, then another. First one wheel was rolling, then the other. The whole seemed in confusion and violent disorder. The vision was terrible to him. The wheels were so high that they were dreadful. But he saw them full of eyes round about. They saw perfectly whither they were going. The objects to be accomplished were clear and understood. Though the motions were so rapid and majestic that they overwhelmed and confounded the feeble vision and thought of the captive, still every thing moved so intelligently and orderly that there could be no real confusion and no mistake. They must prosper in the thing whereto they were sent. They must fulfill the will of God.

This was the wonderful, varied providence of God; a great scheme, full of arrangements, like wheels and wings moving in every direction, and yet all under the control of infinite wisdom and power. This is the same wonderful providence always. What a blessing it is, to be in the hands of such a Being, and under the guidance and care of such protection! All his ways are perfect. He can do in all things according to his will. But he can do no wrong to those who love and trust him. For them all things work together for good, strange and contradictory as they may often appear. God, even their own God, will give them his blessing. He will keep them in perfect peace, and become their salvation, however his whirlwinds and his fire may overturn and consume the plans of men.

But Ezekiel learned, in his vision, another lesson still. In this gracious and wonderful scheme all providences have a secret purpose of blessing for those who love God. Thus David teaches us, "He that dwelleth in the secret place of the Most High, shall abide under the shadow of the Almighty." "The spirit of the living creature was in the wheels, and whithersoever the spirit was to go, they went, thither was their spirit to go." This is a very precious lesson. The plans of divine providence are always subservient to the plans of divine grace.

They follow the guidance of the Holy Spirit. They are designed as blessings for the chosen people of God. Whom he loves, he protects and prospers. There can be no one to harm those who are followers after that which is good. This is true in the life of each of them, and true in the history of the whole. However God may try his people on the way, and however dark, unintelligible, and hard to bear, these trials may appear, the triumphant and happy result is always the same, perfectly sure, and entirely compensating. He refines his chosen ones like gold and silver, and they glorify him in the fires. Whithersoever his converting and renewing Spirit is to go, thither the living wheels and agents of his providence move also, and after he has carried them through the heaviness of the trial, they "are found unto praise and honor and glory at the appearing of Jesus Christ, whom having not seen, they love, and in whom believing, they rejoice with joy unspeakable and full of glory."

We may not be able to interpret all the plans of God on the way. We may be often cast down by the appearance of the approaching judgment. But when his plans are finished, and his purposes are revealed, we see that "the triumphing of the wicked is short, and the joy of the hypocrite is but for a moment;" but "the righteous shall be in everlasting remembrance," and God will never forsake those who trust in him. Such honor, at last, will have all his saints.

Last of all, the captive was taught that all the providences of God are under the control of the great Redeemer and Saviour of the people of God, the Lord Jesus Christ. The government of the world is on his shoulder, and he upholdeth all things by the word of his power. When Ezekiel had seen all this wonderful display of the providence and government of God, he saw in the heavens above "the appearance of a throne like a sapphire stone." Upon the throne was the likeness as of a man sitting. The glorious Ruler over all appeared to him as an incarnate Lord, manifested in the likeness of man, as he was to become under the gospel dispensation. This was a revelation of the only-begotten Son of God. All the intervening providences connected with Israel were to promote this great result of the Saviour's revelation. They were to work together to bring out to view the Redeemer's person, the Redeemer's kingdom, and the Redeemer's throne. The captivity and restoration of Israel were for this great end. The trials and the protection which the captives should receive were to prepare for this result. This future manifestation and work of the appointed Saviour was the great lesson taught under all the revelations of the Old Testament. All the parts and events of these previous dispensations were intended to witness of the coming Saviour, and to lead the hearts of men in faith and hope to him.

This is still the plan and purpose of God. All providences are designed to lead the soul to Christ; to bring the sinful heart and mind of man to the throne of Jesus. God would set up that throne in our hearts. By the indwelling power of his Holy Spirit he would bring our hearts into complete subjection to his power and grace. Blessed are all his providences which can be made the divine instruments of this great result. And blessed are we if they can be permitted to produce this happy result for us.

As we contemplate and experience these gracious providences, let us seek constantly to gain this inestimable blessing, an everlasting portion with the Lord Jesus. As we proceed to consider the history of providence in the captive orphan of Israel, we must do it with this end in constant view. Thus we shall see the principles of instruction, which were given in the captive's vision, brought into actual operation in a captive's history. To us the study may be made a precious blessing. Let us learn to repose upon our Saviour's providence with an affectionate faith; to trust ourselves and all our interests, for time and for eternity, to that glorious Saviour. He will lead us in his own way. He will save us by his own power. He will bless us in his own kingdom. He is all our salvation. And if we truly love him, and trust him, and follow him, we shall be found to the praise of his glory, in having thus in thankful faith put on the Lord Jesus Christ.

III.

The Ruler of the Kingdoms.

"The Most High ruleth in the kingdom of men, and giveth it to whomsoever he will."—Daniel, iv. 25.

WHILE Ezekiel was a captive by the river of Chebar, there was also another distinguished Jewish captive in the city of Babylon. The captive at Chebar was a priest in Israel. The captive in Babylon was one of "the king's seed." They were both made instructors to their nation in the ways and will of God. Ezekiel learned the great principles of divine Providence as he meditated in the open field, especially in connection with the history of Israel. Daniel was instructed by the same great teacher, in these same principles, in their application to the Gentile kingdoms of the world, as he served in the court of Nebuchadnezzar, in Babylon. But they were inspired to speak of the same wonderful providence, and to teach the same unlimited government of God over all. Whether it was the kingdom of Judah, or the kingdom of Babylon, whether they were the people of God or their oppressors to whom attention might be particularly turned, one great truth must never be forgotten. The Most High was equally ruling in all the kingdoms of men, and giving them to whomsoever he would.

Seventy years were to finish the captivity of Israel in Babylon. And when the seventy years were accomplished Babylon was to be conquered, and Israel was to be restored. All this was finished in Daniel's own time. Another whirlwind out of the north came down upon Babylon itself. The Medes and Persians overthrew the kingdom of Nebuchadnezzar, took possession of the city of Babylon, and established the kingdom of Persia on the same territory and over the same people. You are so familiar with all the circumstances of this wonderful conquest and revolution, that I need not enlarge upon them here. They are described in holy Scripture as a remarkable illustration of the mighty providence of God; and these descriptions are given that men might acknowledge and remember this great and unchanging truth, that "the Most High ruleth in the kingdom of men, and giveth it to whomsoever he will."

One of the first acts of Cyrus when he established this new dominion, was to give liberty to all the captive Israelites in his kingdom to return to their homes. His proclamation was, "Who is there among you of all his people? His God be with him. Let him go up to Jerusalem, which is in Judah, and build the house of the Lord God of Israel (He is the God) which is in Jerusalem." A portion of the Jews took advantage of this permission. But many, who had become settled in various ways in the land of their captivity, chose to remain. The gracious providence of God was equally displayed in guiding and protecting the few and feeble people who returned to Palestine, and in the care and government of those who remained in Persia. As years went by, the cloud still unfolded itself. The wheel in the middle of the wheel rolled on also, and God's covenant goodness to the children of his servants was exercised in various plans of benefit for them.

Seventy years more in the history of Israel in Persia bring us to the period of the captive orphan whose story we are now to study. We come to the reign of Artaxerxes Longimanus as he is called in history, and Ahasuerus as he is styled in the holy Scripture. And now all the principles of divine teaching which Ezekiel learned are manifested in new operations of the same divine providence. The Most High is still ruling in the kingdom of men. God is yet maintaining a divine protection and watchfulness over the feeblest and poorest of his saints.

The book of Esther is a story of this wonderful providence of God; providence guarding the interests and defending the security of those who love him; providence disappointing and overturning the craft and malice of those who hate him; providence making all things work together for good to the children of God, and causing the wrath of man to praise him. We have seen the cloud constantly unfolding itself; the wreathed flames separating one after another, until all is clear and bright as amber. We see the whirlwind rushing to destroy, and the living agents of the divine will coming forth, moving before us like the flashing lightning, producing new and unexpected changes in the scene, in connection with which they are displayed, and also combining to accomplish the perfect will of God. We see, at last, the perfect manifestation brought out, of that gracious Saviour whose throne is over all, and who governs all things according to his own will. This is the subject of study in the history of Esther, the captive orphan of Israel.

By this providence of God, I mean here just that which Daniel describes in our present text, the government of the Most High ruling in the kingdoms of men, protecting and exalting his faithful people, and overturning and destroying the power of all who oppose and injure them. Ezekiel's vision pictured this providence to the captive Israelites, and Daniel's interpretation declared its certainty to the king of Babylon.

This providence of God is a secret government. Its great ruler and director is not seen by men. But the results and influence of his presence and power are constantly felt. "The wind bloweth where it listeth, and we hear the sound thereof. But we can not tell whence it cometh, or whither it goeth." Thus the Almighty God ruleth in the affairs of men. While they think only of accomplishing their own plans, they are really finishing his designs, and doing his will. He said to Pharaoh, the cruel king of Egypt, "In very deed, for this cause have I raised thee up, for to show in thee my power, and that my name may be declared throughout all the earth." He calls the Assyrian king "the rod of his anger, and the staff of his indignation," and tells him he "will put a hook in his nose, and a bridle in his lips, and will turn him back by the way by which he came." He warns him that "the axe should not boast itself against him that heweth therewith, nor the saw magnify itself against him that shaketh it." Thus God rules secretly over all, effectually restraining those who oppose him, and constantly protecting those who trust in him, by a providence which is wholly secret in its operation, and manifested only in its results.

This providence of God is a foreseeing government. God foresees all that can occur in the experience and history of his creatures; and thus prepares for all. He provides beforehand the remedy for the sufferings which his servants must bear, and the protection required by the dangers through which they will pass. He overrules the ways and the purposes of men, to bring out his own ends in every thing they do. Whatever they may intend, "the Lord shall rise up, that he may do his work, his strange work, and bring to pass his act, his strange act." Wicked men are often allowed to pursue their own plans until they find themselves to have been entirely defeated in their designs, and to have promoted the very ends they were trying to overthrow. God makes the very things which would appear to be for the hurt, perhaps for the ruin of his people, turn out for the establishment of their welfare and happiness. All this he does by his providence,—"the wheel in the middle of the wheel,"

—foreseeing the evil, and preparing an adequate remedy before it can come to pass.

This providence of God is always designed for the happiness of those who love him. To them he will show the blessings of his covenant, that is, the blessings which will arise to them from being thus under the covenanted protection of their God. He has prepared blessings for those who love him, which pass man's understanding. He makes their faithful obedience to him profitable in all things unto them, having the promise of the life that now is, and of the life that is to come. In whatever trials or dangers they may be for a season, they never fail to see in the end how blessed and how happy it is for them to have the Lord for their God.

This secret providence of God does not exhibit itself habitually in remarkable things. Its operations are not out of the line of man's common experience, and manifested in events which are called miraculous by men. It consists in making the most natural events produce appointed, and sometimes most unexpected results, results entirely opposite to those which men have desired and purposed to attain. While we see one wheel rolling forward, and are looking to the direction in which it appears to be moving with great rapidity and force, suddenly, to our astonishment, the other one starts, and the whole result is found to be entirely opposite to the fears and hopes which we had entertained. The enemy of a good man assaulted him in the night, and attempted to kill him with a sword. But the sword was made to open a secret abscess which no surgeon could reach, under which the man had long suffered, and simply relieving his suffering instead of destroying his life, restored him to health.

We can never surely predict the results of this divine Providence. But we may always know and trust that God will be a sure fortress and refuge to those who love him. Because they have made the Lord their habitation, there shall no evil befall them, neither shall any plague come nigh their dwelling. God will set them on high because they have known his name. Of this we may be always sure.

Events will often come out very far from our fears and expectations. While we are looking at the opening cloud, and point to the direction in which the living creatures are moving, suddenly, without turning, they rush to another quarter, and all our plans are disappointed. This may mark the whole course of these providences in their particular facts, but always in the end we find that it is well for them who fear God.

This is a general view of the working of this divine Providence of which we speak. In the principles which govern its operation it is everywhere the same. It is always true that the triumphing of the wicked is short, and that the blessing of the Lord is in the habitation of the righteous. This general view may teach us to wait with patience until we see what the Lord will do; to be quiet, and silence all our complaints and fears, while he is perfecting and revealing his will; to be believing, trusting in his mind and affection towards all who love him; to be faithful and persevering in our appointed duty, without concern for any of its possible results; to glorify God in the midst of the fires; and never, never to doubt, that God will bring out the utmost happiness for his people, and the utmost glory for himself, from all his work, when he has finished and exhibited its full results.

The history of Esther and her cotemporaries displays this gracious and governing providence in a very clear and remarkable manner. It does this both in the general subject of the history, and in the particular events which occur in its course. Each of these events seems perfectly natural and likely to occur. They are all entirely adapted to the characters with which they are connected. Each person acts just as such persons would be likely to act in such circumstances. But every event results entirely contrary to the plans and expectations of those who were engaged in them. Every thing seems to be ordered by a secret power, which is overruling all, restraining all, directing all, and making them all to accomplish that which this divine power directs. Man proposes, but God disposes. Man "meaneth not so, neither doth his heart think so. It is in his heart to destroy. He saith, by the strength of my hand I have done it, and by my wisdom, for I am prudent." But God shows him that even "the king's heart is in the hand of the Lord; as the rivers of water, he turneth it whithersoever he will," and "he giveth the kingdom to whomsoever he will."

There is hardly a single great principle of religious or moral truth which may not be illustrated from the history of Esther. Its characters and its events are in the highest degree significant and instructive. The circumstances of trial through which all its actors are carried, combine to present one of the most beautiful and impressive exhibitions of God's great goodness to his children—of his faithfulness to his promises, of his certain protection of them from the hands of the ungodly, and of their final acknowledgment and exaltation in his favor.

The providence of God teaches man four great lessons. All others may be considered as included in these four. These lessons are the four which it is most important for man to learn and understand. They are taught in the whole line of human history, and in the constant observation and experience of individual men. They are, the emptiness of the present world as a portion for man, the temporary, short-lived triumphs of human wickedness, the certain security of those who love God in all the dangers of earth, and the sure happiness and reward of a life of obedience and devotion to him. These four great lessons are taught in every generation and in every land, where the children of God are disposed to study and consider them. They are taught on a larger or a smaller scale, as we contemplate the history of multitudes, in long periods of time, or as we consider the lives of individuals illustrative of each particular lesson.

These four great lessons God wishes to teach to each of you, in his whole system of personal government over you, and by the light and guidance of his gracious Spirit within you. He arranges for you the day of prosperity, that you may be joyful, and the day of adversity that you may consider. And he sets the one over against the other to the end that man should find nothing after him. His whole scheme is perfect, and leaves nothing unnoticed or unprovided for, that he who is taught in it of God may be wise unto salvation through faith in Jesus Christ.

My dear young friends, this is the great purpose of divine instruction in the providence of God. He would show you the emptiness of the present world as a portion, that he may lead you off from its vain and ruinous pursuits, and persuade you to seek the things above, where Jesus sitteth at the right hand of God. He would show you the miserable disappointments which attend the designs of wicked and crafty men, however cunningly devised, that he may lead you away from the temptations which gather around the path of the ungodly, and persuade you to have no fellowship with them. He would show you the abiding safety of those who love and trust him, that he may attract your hearts to them, and induce you to walk in the happy paths which they have chosen. He would show you the certain happiness and reward of a life of obedience and virtue, of usefulness to men and piety to God, that he may encourage you to walk in their steps, and to be followers of them, even as they are of Christ. In this whole scheme of divine teaching you are made to see and "know that it shall be well with them that fear God; but it shall not be well with the wicked, neither shall he prolong his days, which are as a shadow, because he feareth not before God."

These are the teachings of the Holy Spirit in your study of the government of God. They are lessons which you can really learn only by his power. The Psalmist says he could not understand them "until he went into the sanctuary of God." There he found that the ungodly are brought into desolation, as in a moment; they are utterly consumed with terrors; but that those who love God, he "guides by his counsel, and afterwards receiveth them to glory." Thus his final choice and decision was, "Whom have I in heaven but thee? and there is none upon the earth I desire besides thee."

What instruction can you need which these

great lessons do not contain? They cover the whole line of human welfare and destiny. They offer you an adequate strength and guide in life, and a portion of blessedness for ever. All other knowledge is worthless in comparison with this. The more deeply and practically you understand it, the wiser and the happier do you become. But none can teach you all this save the Holy Spirit of God. He opens to you the book of providence. Under his guidance you will see the true light, your souls will embrace the blessed hope, and you will rejoice in the treasures of grace and glory, which are to be found in Jesus Christ our Lord.

IV.

The Great Lesson.

"Let us hear the conclusion of the whole matter: fear God, and keep his commandments, for this is the whole of man."—ECCLESIASTES, xii. 13.

THIS was the great lesson which the royal preacher learned after much experience. He gained it as the result of many efforts at enjoyment and many trials. Happy would it have been for him had he acquired this important lesson in the beginning of his life, and avoided all the sins and sorrows which taught it to him in the end. His venerable father, in his own dying hours, had impressed upon him the interest and duty of loving and serving the God of his fathers: "And thou Solomon, my son, know thou the God of thy fathers, and serve him with a perfect heart and a willing mind, for the Lord searcheth all hearts, and understandeth all imaginations of the thoughts; if thou seek him, he will be found of thee; if thou forsake him, he will cast thee off for ever."

But Solomon rejected his father's counsel, and forsook the God of his fathers. He tried a life of sensual enjoyment and disobedience to God. He gratified his tastes with intellectual attainments, and with magnificent display. And at the close of a wasted and sinful life, he sums up all his acquisitions of earthly gain and folly, as vanity and vexation of spirit. He gives us as the result of his whole experience, and the final choice and decision of his heart, the lesson of our text: "Fear God, and keep his commandments, for this is the whole of man."

This is the great practical lesson of holy Scripture. The object of all its instruction is to persuade man in his youth to choose the love and favor of God, to be reconciled in heart to him as a gracious Saviour, and to make him his portion for ever. For this God has given his own dear Son, and sent forth his Holy Spirit, to open a way in which our sinful souls might be brought back to him in peace, and walk in that new and living way, in holy obedience to him for ever.

This is the great lesson, also, which the divine providence teaches. In whatever part of the government of God you study his holy will, you will find him leading you to the same important truth. The providence of God is a great and effectual school for man, in which the word and the Spirit of God become his teachers. They show him there a thousand lessons, by which they would impress the great truth upon his mind, "the favor of God, that is life, and his loving-kindness is better than life." This lesson is for him "the conclusion of the whole matter." When this has been thoroughly learned, the education of man in the school of providence has been completed.

As a school for man the scheme of divine Providence has four different chambers of instruction, in which this same great lesson is taught to man from four different subjects of contemplation. I have before called them four different lessons. But they are rather four different aspects of one lesson, that one lesson which our text declares to be the conclusion of the whole matter of human experience, and the whole interest and duty of man for time and for eternity.

First, there is the chamber of sensual enjoyment. There the Holy Spirit teaches us that all is emptiness and disappointment. Myriads of instances and specimens are employed to illustrate the lesson. But the facts which they are made to prove are always the same.

Second, there is the chamber of human wickedness. There the Spirit teaches us that all the plans of the ungodly result in failure and ruin. Every circumstance of advantage is conceded to them. But the issue is everywhere and in every case the same.

Third, there is the chamber of true piety towards God. There the Spirit teaches us that there is certain security and everlasting blessedness. Millions of individuals are brought forward as instances, a multitude which no man can number. But their testimony is uniform and unchanging. "Their way is a way of pleasantness, and all their paths are peace."

Fourth, there is the chamber of active usefulness to men. In this the Spirit teaches us that there is always a sure success, and a glorious, satisfying reward. Every nation presents its illustrations. Every age produces its testimony. But there is no diversity in the experience. "Mark the perfect man, and behold the upright, for the end of that man is peace." "Light is sown for the righteous, and joyful gladness for the upright in heart."

In these chambers of observation, four classes in the school of providence are arranged. When we have passed through them all, and have acquired the four lessons which are there taught, our education is complete. We have been graduated in this divine school, and have completely learned the lesson of our text. In the conviction of our judgments at least, when we have come to the conclusion of the whole matter of human experience on earth, we all learn it. And if the Holy Spirit has truly led our hearts to fear and obey the Lord, whose ways we have studied, and to keep his commandments with a perfect heart, we have then learned all that the limits of this life can teach, and all that our happiness and security for eternity can require.

The BOOK OF ESTHER, the history of the CAPTIVE ORPHAN, is a beautiful exhibition of this divine school, with its four chambers of instruction. It is the history of a complete course of teaching in living illustrations. It is spread out before us, as a microcosm, a world in itself, with specimens of all the variety of facts which make up the great world abroad, completely displayed. It is a succession of tableaux, in which every phase of human society is successively displayed; a series of dissolving views, which, as they succeed each other, give new and separate lessons on the great subject which they are all combined to teach. And as each is successively completed, we feel more and more ready to say, " Let us hear the conclusion of the whole matter; fear God and keep his commandments, for this is the whole of man."

This series of views opens with the earth triumphant, wickedness exalted, virtue prostrate and piety concealed. It goes on in its dissolving and reconstructing process, until it closes with the world cast down, wickedness overthrown, virtue and religion reigning and the heavenly kingdom supreme. What lessons can be more important than these? They are successive manifestations of the truth and purposes of God. They are the great facts which the Holy Spirit teaches in all the pages of the word of God. They are the lessons which he would write effectually on every human heart. But they are all parts of the one great lesson of our text, "Fear God and keep his commandments, for this is the whole of man," of every man, wherever, whoever, whatever he may be. No man living can ever learn more; no man living has ever learned any thing to profit who has not learned this. It is the great lesson of earth. It is the great law of heaven.

In this remarkable story, the divine teacher takes us first into the chamber of sensual enjoyment. There every thing is displayed on the grandest scale. He shows us earthly magnificence and splendor in the highest degree and in every variety of arrangement. Never was human pomp more gorgeous. Never were means and provisions for indulgence richer or more abundant. Never was there a fairer chance for human happiness, if mere sensual pleasure can ever give happiness to man. The experiment is fairly made and under the most advantageous conditions. But it is all in vain. The grand display ends in disappointment, degradation and crime. The result is misery and conscious loss. Even royal magnificence leaves the soul completely empty. It is all vanity and vexation of spirit. It is " as when a hungry man dreameth, and behold he eateth; but he awaketh, and his soul is empty." "The fashion of this world passeth away."

This is the first great lesson in the divine providence. It is a lesson which every one must learn for himself, and which many learn through much disappointment and trial. This present world as a portion is thoroughly unsatisfying and vain. Enlarge it as you will, enrich it as you will, it will yield nothing in the end to the soul that loves it most. It is a broken reed, which will only pierce the hand that leans upon it. The Holy Spirit would teach you this as his first great lesson on every scale of trial which the providence of God may allow. Rich or poor, great or small, young or old, all that you see, all that you can get out of the earth will never fill your wants. The child may throw away his broken toy—the merchant may contemplate with dismay his argosies wrecked—the statesman may see his dreams of honor ending in disgrace—Alexander may weep that there are no more worlds to conquer—the bubbles and speculations of men burst, and their investments put forth unsuspected wings and fly away. The lesson is everywhere the same. The utter emptiness of the world as a portion for man, is that which they all severally teach. He is the happiest who learns the lesson the soonest, and with the least amount of sorrow in the experience which impresses it. Learn it, sooner or later every living man must, whether he desire it or not; and the sooner and the easier they learn it, the happier will it be for all.

The great teacher next introduces us into the chamber of true piety towards God. He shows us a lovely and helpless orphan. She is poor, an exile, a captive, and beautiful in the highest degree. She is exposed to all the temptations which surround such a child of loveliness and innocence in a world of licentiousness and crime. Her parents called her their myrtle (Hadassah) in the beauty of her infancy. Her admirers proclaimed her a star (Esther) in the splendor of her maturity. No condition in human life involves a greater amount of hazard and danger than this. "Ah," said a sister once to me, weeping over orphan loveliness in poverty fallen from virtue, "my poor sister was cursed with beauty." Who has not seen that which will make him feel and understand the force of this bitter exclamation? But the orphan girl before us now, was a child of piety and prayer, one who feared and loved the God of her fathers. She had learned in the very beginning of her life by the Lord's own teaching that great lesson which Solomon calls the whole of man, and she is preserved by it from destruction and sin in the very midst of all the arts and cruelties of the wicked. There is a divine watchfulness and care over her, which never fails. Her father and her mother have forsaken her, but the God of her fathers has taken her up. She is safe in the midst of snares on every side. She is raised to the highest point of earthly dignity, influence and usefulness. She becomes an instrument of blessing to thousands of her own countrymen, and a mother to her nation. She closes her career in triumph and happiness.

This is another great lesson in the school of providence. The Holy Spirit teaches it in every generation and on every scale. Happy are they who truly learn it. The favor of God, that is life. True piety towards God is always true prosperity under God. However poor it may be in the outset, it is never forsaken. God brings forth its righteousness as clear as the light, and its just dealing as the noon day. Its difficulties all vanish. Crooked things before it are made straight. The Lord is its light and its salvation, and there is none of whom it need be afraid. The exhibition of this great truth is a blessed lesson indeed. Happy are they who learn it, and adopt the guidance and encouragement which it imparts, in their earliest youth. To them God becomes a portion for ever.

Next, the great teacher takes us into the chamber of human wickedness. It is a terrible manifestation of what may be found in the heart of a sinful man. It is malicious and crafty, unscrupulous and powerful. It has every possible advantage on its side; wealth, power and abundant opportunity. All unite to secure its entire success. Its triumph seems inevitable. But its success would be the destruction of the godly whom the Lord loveth. We watch its unfolding purposes of cruelty and wasting. So perfect is the machinery employed, that we see not how their accomplishment is to be avoided. Suddenly there starts "a wheel in the middle of a wheel." The wicked is allowed to go on, until he is caught in his own snares. He has been providing for his own destruction. He falls into the very pit he had been digging for others. God overturns all his schemes in a most unexpected, but in a perfectly natural manner. The train of opposition which this providence has laid, begins afar off. The wicked man is shooting forward his mine underground until he has arrived as he imagines beneath the very residence which he means to destroy. He is ready to apply his torch. In another hour, he says, my hated enemy will be destroyed. But God has been countermining beneath him all the while, and just as he is about to fire his train, the opposite one is touched, and his whole work exploded. The wicked is driven away in his wickedness, and the righteous cometh in his stead. Nothing could be more simple than this overthrow of the ungodly. Nothing could be more wonderful. Nothing could be more complete.

But what a lesson this is! "Though hand join in hand," says God, "the wicked shall not go unpunished." "Though the sinner do evil a thousand times, yet we know that it shall be well with them that fear God, but it shall not be well with the wicked." Where was this great lesson ever taught in a manner more striking or more solemn than in this story! It is a lesson of fearful warning to the sinner, but of great encouragement to those who trust in God. And it is of unspeakable importance to us all, to learn it thoroughly and to be thoroughly convinced of its truth.

The great teacher takes us lastly into the chamber of human virtue and usefulness to men. It is clouded with many difficulties. The illustrating object is a poor, unnoticed man, sitting on the door-steps of the great and wicked. He is the object of virulent persecution and hostility. He has no means of defense. The apparent certainty in his prospect is absolute destruction by the combined power of his enemies. But he is calm, faithful and determined. "He that believeth shall not make haste." So it proves here. The virtue and usefulness which mark this illustration move forward without fear, in their chosen and appointed path. An unseen God wonderfully interposes. Virtue is made to triumph in doing right, and simply by doing right. It is generous and unflinching in its fidelity, and it is protected and made successful in its career. It is recompensed with power, honor and influence. It gains the very honor which persecuting wickedness had ingeniously planned for itself, and it sees the very punishment which it had been doomed to suffer, inflicted upon its bitter persecutor. It triumphs completely. It is made a blessing and protection to the multitude of its own nation. In the beautiful language of this history at its close, its possessor abides, " accepted of the multitude of his brethren, seeking the wealth of his people, and speaking peace to all his seed." Nothing could be more triumphant. God has vindicated all his purposes, and all his plans are clear and finished. Man can find nothing in coming after him. And when we come out of this chamber, we find the same truth displayed in the living experience of men, everywhere, and in all the circumstances of life. It is always well with those who love God.

These are the four chambers of instruction, and the four successive exhibitions of truth in this great school of providence, as they are displayed in the history of the CAPTIVE ORPHAN. They are the four lessons which the providence of God everywhere teaches upon the varying scale of human experience. They combine to illustrate the whole moral government of God among men. They are parts of the one great lesson, which our text declares to be the whole of man. When man has been taught by the Holy Spirit these important lessons, so that the choice of the heart and the course of life have been formed and governed by their influence, there is nothing more for man to learn upon earth. His education is completed. The great purpose of his earthly being is finished. He has then found a treasure in a reconciled God, a portion for the soul in the complete forgiveness and acceptance which the Saviour offers, an inheritance of blessedness and glory in his presence, and he will be guided by the Holy Spirit, the Comforter, through a life of faithfulness to God, to its possession and enjoyment.

Happy are you, my dear young friends, if you early learn this great fourfold lesson, under the Saviour's guidance and by the teaching of his Holy Spirit. Happier far, the sooner and the more effectually you acquire it. These are the lessons which the story of the CAPTIVE ORPHAN is designed to teach; and if you really study and learn these there, Esther will be made a blessing to you, as she was made a blessing to her own nation and its posterity. Seek in the whole course of your study of her history for that divine teaching, without which the providence of God seems only confusion, and the word of God a sealed and unintelligible book. Under this teaching you will gain new wisdom and grace in every step of your own life, and in every observation of the lives of others. Thus you will love and justify your gracious God in all his dealings with you or others. Thus you will be made ready to understand, and to unite in that triumphant song of the saints in glory, "Great and marvelous are thy works, Lord God Almighty. Just and true are all thy ways, thou King of saints."

V.

The First Experience.

"Vanity of vanities, saith the preacher; vanity of vanities; all is vanity."—
ECCLESIASTES, I. 2.

THUS we enter the school of providence. It opens for us in the chamber of this world, in its provisions for sensual enjoyment. And the first lesson we are taught, is the complete emptiness of earthly joy as a portion for man.

To teach us the same lesson, Solomon describes his experiments as a preacher for others. He recounts all his observations of the world, and all his plans in the world, the indulgences and the gains which he had gotten and seen, the means of gratification which he possessed, and his ardor in the use of them, and then tells us, in our text, the estimate in which all his experience had resulted.

What he discovered in this bitter experience of disappointment, all who pursue the same course will also find. In whatever degree or on whatever scale the world is chosen for a portion, bitter disappointment will be the result. The harvest will be but one heap of sorrow in the end. "He that soweth to the flesh, shall of the flesh reap corruption." Its gains and pleasures can never give content to the heart of man. And the royal preacher has given us this sad history of his own experience under the guidance of the Holy Spirit, to warn off all succeeding navigators from the rocks on which he made his shipwrecks, and the shoals, in the bosom of which he found himself engulfed.

With a history of such an experiment, the story of Esther begins. The first view is earthly magnificence ending in disappointment and vanity. The trial of the fullest sufficiency of earth is displayed. The arrangements are upon a scale including the utmost conceivable preparations for gratification, and the most entire reality of sensual enjoyment. Never can the pleasures of the world be more fairly tried. If under any circumstances they can give real delight, they must give it here. Nothing of the glory of earth is wanting in the picture which we here contemplate.

First, there is unlimited power. The man presented to our view is "reigning from India even unto Ethiopia, over an hundred and seven and twenty provinces." He is the ruler of the great Persian empire, established by Cyrus, and enlarged by his successors. It included the whole vast empire of Babylon, and a still wider extension of dominion. The king who is personally brought before us here is Artaxerxes Longimanus, the son of the celebrated Xerxes. He came to the throne amidst rival competitors of great power. In many victorious battles he overthrew all these competitors to his kingdom, and was the undisputed possessor of the Persian throne.

He is introduced to us in the third year of his reign, about four hundred and sixty-two years before the advent of our Lord, when he had secured a full and peaceable possession of the whole empire, and ruled without an opposer or a rival.

His power was supreme. The life of every

subject in his kingdom depended on his word. He ruled without resistance and without control. So far as men were concerned, he did according to his own will, and there was no one to dispute or question his right. His hundred and twenty-seven provinces were the very center and garden of the world. They included the beautiful plains and rivers of Central and Western Asia, from the Mediterranean to the Indus, from "India to Ethiopia;" in the most healthful and perfect climate of the world. They were inhabited by the most crowded, and the richest population of the globe. When this monarch went abroad he was an object of supreme veneration. Men prostrated themselves before him as if he were divine. The wealth, the productions, the inhabitants of the greatest empire of the earth, were thus his undisputed right. "All people, nations and languages trembled and feared before him: whom he would he slew; and whom he would he left alive. Whom he would he set up; and whom he would he put down." Thus Ahasuerus reigned in triumphant power and glory, when the view before us was taken.

Here was one great object of human ambition completely gained. What struggles are made on earth for the attainment of office and personal dominion! We read of them in the annals of every nation, and in all the pages of human history. The lust of power has waged the deadliest wars of earth, excited the cruelest murders of men, and deluged nations with blood. "Every battle of the warrior with its confused noise, and garments rolled in blood," has been one in the list of innumerable evidences of what man will do and bear in the violent determination to rule. Among ourselves we see this lust of power on a smaller scale, in all the political efforts, and contested elections of our own day, and in our own land. What toils and tricks, what extravagance of expense and wasteful indulgences, what time, and labor, and crimes, are devoted under our eyes, to this struggle for human power! Men in multitudes are ready to sacrifice every thing which ought to be dear to man, for the attainment of a far inferior measure of human power than Ahasuerus peaceably enjoyed. And with a glowing exhibition of man's favorite aspect of the present world, the possession of unlimited power, our series of illustrations opens.

Second, there is a peaceful and secure possession of this unlimited power. The view is given to us "in those days when Ahasuerus sat on the throne of his kingdom." All is quiet around him, and every thing is ready to minister to his enjoyment. His father's life had been spent in warfare. The stories of the conquests and the defeats of Xerxes are familiar to you from childhood. Ahasuerus possessed his father's dominions in perfect peace. He had nothing to do but to govern peacefully and to enjoy abundantly. We find him "on the throne of his kingdom which was in Shushan, the palace," contemplating his victories past, his present possessions, and his possible enjoyments and pleasures.

The city of Shushan, or Susa, was founded by Cyrus for his royal residence. Daniel says, "I was at Shushan in the palace." It was adopted by the kings of Persia for their winter abode.

It stood on the banks of the river Ulai, and was remarkable for its beauty and its attractive winter climate. It was called Shushan, a lily, perhaps from the beauty of its architecture, or from the rapid growth in the richness and glory of its display, springing up like a beautiful lily on the river bank, and the lily was adopted, and is still to be seen among its carved remains, as its chosen distinguishing symbol. Here, amidst all the joys of unlimited power, peace and wealth, Ahasuerus reigned. What blessings he might have dispersed abroad! What monuments of usefulness to men he might have established!

The peaceful possession of power is a great privilege, as well as a great temptation. It enables man to be a benefactor to his race. He may sit as a king among the mourners and make a thousand weary hearts to sing for joy. But it is a great temptation to the sensual cupidity of man. It may make him, in a terrific degree, an oppressor of his fellow men for his own gain. And unless God is pleased to interpose with his own guiding and sustaining Spirit, there is but little likelihood that man will resist the temptation to his own selfishness. The history of the world is filled with the stories of human power oppressive and destructive. But ah, how few have been the illustrations of the same power beneficent and protecting! Yet this peaceful possession of great power is a tempting exhibition of the world. It shines out as an element of great attraction and ornament, and in the view before us it is remarkably displayed.

Third, there is the possession of vast wealth and outward glory. Ahasuerus gathered around him "all his princes, his servants, the power of Persia, and Media, the nobles and princes of the provinces being before him, when he showed the riches of his glorious kingdom and the honor of his excellent majesty." Probably there was never a greater accumulation of wealth in proportion to the gratifications it would purchase. The riches of Xerxes were beyond the computation of man, and all these and more than these were in the hands of his successor. All this incalculable wealth was concentrated in the hands of an individual ruler. He could do with it as he pleased. He could expend it without accountability to any one. No condition could appear to an earthly mind more desirable or tempting.

We know something of the struggle for wealth. It is the great object for contest in the peaceful walks of business and commercial enterprise. To be rich, in modern society, is to be influential and exalted. Money is considered the great element of power, and we are familiar with the toils and earnestness of self-denial and labor which men will habitually bear to accomplish the attainment of this chosen object. But in the picture before us, there is wealth which would be esteemed as a fabulous calculation and an impossible attainment by the wildest speculators of our day. Its hundredth part would be to us an inheritance beyond what the most ambitious commerce imagines within its reach. It was an unlimited ability to purchase all the happiness which the world could give, in its utmost provisions for sensual enjoyment.

What a vast privilege is the possession of such wealth! What happiness it may communicate when it is faithfully dispensed and employed as an instrument for human benefit! How great is the honor and the joy of being thus a public benefactor to mankind! But the responsibility is also great. Alas, how opposite to all this is the habitual use of wealth! It leads the selfish mind to a forgetfulness and neglect of the wants of others. It persuades sinful men that they have the right to live for their own indulgence and pleasure, and are not to be held responsible to others for the way in which their own acquisitions and means of influence are employed. But though wealth may be desired, and too often used for mere selfish gratification, it is still the great object of human desire and human labor. The possession of it is still the great ornament and attraction of the world. In the view before us, its amount transcended all the habitual calculations of man concerning it. And in this element, all that the world could ask to be conceded is allowed.

Fourth, here is also splendid display. Wealth is often hoarded with a covetous grasp for mere accumulation. Man wants even the openness of heart for its display. But in the picture by which the Holy Spirit will illustrate for us the emptiness of the world, there shall be no such defect. The wealth which has been amassed shall have the opportunity of the utmost manifestation. Accordingly, the glory of this display transcends our imagination. All the riches of fabled Eastern magnificence are here actually combined. The court of the garden of the king's palace is laid open to our view. Gold and silver couches are spread abroad. The richest silken tapestry is seen suspended in curtains of beauty, of every variety of color and pattern. Pillars of marble stand to hold, with silver rings, this gorgeous pavilion. Vessels of gold, in every fanciful shape, are provided for the royal guests. Pavements of precious stones are spread beneath their feet. Nothing can exceed the magnificence of this exhibition. "The king made a feast unto all the people who were present in Shushan, the palace, both unto great and small, seven days, in the court of the garden of the king's palace; where were white, green and blue hangings, fastened with cords of fine linen and purple to silver rings and pillars of marble. The beds were of gold and silver, upon a pavement of red and blue and white and black marble. And they gave them drink in vessels of gold, the vessels being diverse one from another, and royal wine in abundance, according to the state of the king." Nothing can be added to this display in the human imagination of this element of mere earthly joy.

And how attractive is such a scene to the eye of man! Its feeblest imitations in any society or nation would draw crowds merely to witness it, and with untiring delight. How we follow after pageants and exhibitions of the lowest kind! The gilded tinsel of such scenes, whether military or dramatic, funereal or joyous, is always exciting and attractive to the giddy, silly minds of the multitude. But the royal splendors of a scene like the one here described few would be able to conceive. Its attractions to the many of those who listen to me would, I fear, have been absorbing. The view would have appeared to them a picture of unmingled and extravagant delight. Nothing could be imagined to transcend it. Yet all this display is freely thrown into the picture of the world, that nothing may appear to be wanting to a fair experiment. There shall be no defect in the magnificence of the preparation to give occasion to any complaint to be subsequently made. The Lord says to you freely, Behold the picture of the world at its brightest. Add to it any thing you can desire or conceive. Withhold your heart in its imaginations from no joy. And you are compelled to answer that you have nothing to add. You acknowledge that the experiment is a fair and noble one.

Fifth, there is not only all this power, wealth and display combined; there is also here boundless actual indulgence and hospitality. First, there is a six months' festival for all the nobles and princes of the empire. This included every variety of game, amusement and exhibition that royal wealth or human ingenuity could devise. The festivals of the Persian kings glow and shine in the descriptions of ancient history. Hunting, riding, archery, races, processions and shows of every kind, taxed the royal means of indulgence and purpose of exaltation and vanity. Thus "Ahasuerus made a feast unto all his princes and servants; the power of Persia and Media, the nobles and princes of the provinces being before him; when he showed the riches of his glorious kingdom, and the honor of his excellent majesty, many days, even an hundred and fourscore days."

When this festival was ended, a feast was also made for the people in Shushan great and small, with an hospitality equally abundant. Vessels of gold were in the hands of all. Royal stores of wine flowed without stint for all who came. Unrestrained liberty was secured to every guest. The king's officers were charged to do according to every man's pleasure. It was a glorious scheme for unlimited indulgence and delight for the gathered multitudes of the people. They drank "royal wine in abundance, according to the state of the king. The drinking was according to the law; none did compel; for so had the king appointed to all the officers of his house, that they should do according to every man's pleasure." "Also Vashti, the queen, made a feast for the women in the royal house which belonged to King Ahasuerus."

What could have been more grand or satisfying in earthly things? Doubtless the whole multitude applauded the magnificence and hospitality of the youthful monarch. If the world can give man happiness in sensual indulgence, here was a scene of its perfect joy. No element of delight is wanting in such a picture. If we should attempt the combination of imaginary elements, such as should make a complete display of the glory of the world, what could we ask which was not there? Unlimited power,—peaceful dominion,—vast accumulation of wealth,—glorious display of its value,—boundless indulgence of its stores in hospitality to all. Is not such an aggregate all of earth? Does it not include every thing which the youthful mind might desire? And this is the scene of worldly grandeur with which the school of providence opens before us in this story. This is the first of those dissolving views by which God would teach us not to "love the world, or the things that are in the world," but to "seek the things which are above where Jesus sitteth at the right hand of God," for "the things which are seen are temporal, but the things which are not seen are eternal."

It is not often indeed that such scenes as are here described can be realized. But they are possible. And certainly in the one which we are contemplating, every thing that the earthly heart could desire was present in the glorious combination. Was not all this sufficient? Could not the heart of man be happy in such abundance? The sequel of the story will show the disappointment. But Solomon tells us the real worth of the whole—" vanity of vanities, all is vanity and vexation of spirit."

All these provisions are unsatisfying still. The heart of man covets something more. Its imaginations and desires grow as they are supplied. No new scene of earthly joy becomes more satisfying than the past. The heart turns from its last enjoyment wearied still. And when you have run the whole possible circuit, you will be just as wearied of the whole.

They are all unsuitable. The soul has other views and needs, which none of these outward provisions of the earth can ever reach. There is still the burden of inward sin. There is still the want of reconciliation to God. There is still the consciousness of an inward and a future life which none of these things can touch. And amidst all the joys which earth can give, the conscience will still cry out under the pressure of guilt, and the soul will still refuse to be deceived, or to be at rest short of the immortality to which it feels its right.

They are temporary. They are the things of a day at the best. The whole of a worldly life is but a day's dream of pleasure. To-morrow it will be over. The hour will come when naked as we came, naked we must also go. There is no durable riches for the soul but the favor of God, and the peace which Jesus gives. Without these, the hour of death is miserable and hopeless. What if you had all the glories of the youthful Artaxerxes? They give no hope of glory in the world to come, no joy to the soul in the hour of its departure. There God is every thing. The world is nothing, and the happy man is the man rich in faith, and heir of the "kingdom to come." All other wealth is but a burden and a snare.

To take you off from this vain pursuit of earth, is the purpose of such a scene as the one we have considered. Look at it, not to desire it, but to discern its vanity. Behold how empty, how unsatisfying, how unsuitable, how transitory it is! Cease to look there for your joys. Build not your habitation there. Lay not up your treasures there. Realize that peace of mind, a heart fixed on Christ, a real living for God by his Spirit, is of infinite worth beyond all that this gay and vain world can give. As you study this first lesson of providence, in the school which we have entered here, lose not the conviction of truth which the lesson is designed to give. Forget not the admonition with which it addresses you: "Depart, depart, this is not your rest." Here "vanity of vanities, all is vanity."

VI.

The Bitter Disappointment.

"Madness is in their hearts while they live."—ECCLESIASTES, ix. 3.

THIS is the simple history of the reason of a sinner's life,—what may be called the philosophy of the world's rebellion. Madness is in their hearts. Never was the testimony more clear or true than in the case of the worldly man, whose experiment of vast indulgence the Holy Spirit has given us in the story of Esther.

In studying the ways of providence in the chamber of the world's indulgence, we have witnessed the experiment which he has tried for us. It was upon a plan of magnificence, and with a variety of provision which have never been exceeded. And the admonition becomes for us still the stronger from its result. No element of earthly gratification was wanting. No defect in the splendor of the arrangement can be detected. If this trial could not prove adequate for the desires of man, surely no provision of mere worldly joy ever can be.

But was it sufficient? Was Ahasuerus contented with what he had so richly enjoyed? Did he adorn his condition of such amazing grandeur with a peaceful and satisfied mind? Nay, the vanity and emptiness of this whole scene of glory we have already seen. "Like the crackling of thorns beneath the pot, so is the mirth of fools." And yet mere emptiness was not all that this experiment exhibited. We have now another view to take. We stand in this chamber of the world to witness a still more remarkable scene of its madness and folly.

First, Behold the thorough dissatisfaction which attends its joys. See the conscious wretchedness which limits all its pleasures. The ancient Egyptians used to place a death's head on their tables of festivity, as a solemn warning to the ungoverned spirit of man's indulgence. Philip of Macedon had a herald to stand behind him at his feasts, sounding the alarming admonition, "Remember, Philip, thou art mortal." But how unnecessary was all this array of paraded warning. God has already established his own herald in the heart of man himself—a herald whose voice can not be silenced, and whose office will never be laid aside while man rebels. Man finds an inherent and inseparable element of dissatisfaction in all the scenes of his earthly joys. They do not, they can not meet his wants. He may multiply and extend his gratifications as he will, there is still a madness in his heart while he lives, which refuses satisfaction with his provisions, and scoffs at all attempts to silence its claims or to still its complaints. The history of all his experiments is written in the prophet's testimony, "He earneth wages to put it into a bag with holes." He grasps what he supposes to be substantial pleasure, and proves it a shadow in his defeated attempt. He awakes always to find that his soul is empty, and sad in the consciousness of the fact.

Ahasuerus is just as unsatisfied with all his magnificent display, and with his six months' pompous festival, as the poorest subject of his realm is with his own hard lot. Unlimited opportunity of indulgence is nothing, while there is a limited capacity to enjoy, and an unlimited craving for enjoyment. In the drunkenness of his festival there still needs some further, higher stretch of power, to gratify the desire for display, and to arouse new admiration of his ability and his means of enjoyment. To a mere worldly mind the supposed envy with which its means of indulgence are contemplated by others is a frequent gratification. You behold vanity lolling in its barouche in your streets, or calling attention to the splendor of its edifices, its furniture, its decorations, its pictures, in your avenues of wealthy abode. How often is the crowning feeling of delight in these possessions, the mere imagination of the envy with which others are supposed to regard them. How tasteless do they become if there are none to admire and to praise!

Crœsus carried Solon through all the magnificence of his palace and his treasures, enjoying the wonder and the admiration he should excite, and then asked the philosopher if he knew any one who was happier than he? It

THE BITTER DISAPPOINTMENT. 99

was the mere utterance of that which is a common consciousness to silly, worldly minds. Their happiness can only live in the applause of their display. The philosopher answered the monarch that he knew a poor man in Athens far happier, for he was perfectly contented with his narrow lot. But what a silent confession is there of disappointment and unhappiness in this passion for admiration. It reveals the self-indulgent man as after all a dependent beggar asking alms from others to fill up the cravings of his want. Such was Ahasuerus. His heart was empty of joy, though filled with madness.

He imagines a new spectacle which will awaken a new admiration. He commands his seven chamberlains " to bring Vashti, the queen, before the king, with the crown royal, to show the people and the princes her beauty, for she was fair to look on." "The heart of the king was merry with wine," and he resolved to exhibit the peerless beauty of his queen to his drunken companions. The beauty of Vashti was doubtless supreme, as her very name, which is "Beauty," imports. And Ahasuerus would degrade her and degrade himself by this public exhibition of her loveliness to the multitude who thronged his courts. But the command was an outrage on the habits and education of a Persian lady, and on the rights and dignity of a wife and a queen. The man who treats his wife with irreverence or disrespect, but exposes and degrades himself. Ahasuerus perhaps would have felt and remembered this at another time. But now "the heart of the king was merry with wine." He was drunk, and the madness which was in his heart would submit to no question or refusal.

He thus openly staked the authority of a Persian king, and he could not allow himself to be disobeyed. The seven chamberlains issue forth from the banquet to bring this lauded beauty to the presence of the king. The command was public, and the gathered multitude looked for its fulfillment. The messengers had gone; they were the mere messengers of the king's discontent, witnesses of the emptiness of worldly mirth. The giddy throng watched the door of entrance to the banquet hall in amazed anticipation of their new delight. The queen whom they never had seen, they were now to gaze at and admire in her womanly and royal splendor all unveiled. The mad brain of the youthful monarch reeled under the excitement of their expectation, and in the anticipation of the envy of his brilliant possession which her appearance would excite. What madness indeed is in his heart, in the desire, and in the scheme of its gratification.

But he is not alone. Where is the feast, or where the provision of the world for human gratification, in which there is nothing left for the heart to desire? or in which the heart actually desires nothing more? Ahasuerus is but a specimen, a type. His folly has been multiplied in myriads of instances, and in every variety in the scale of imitation. It only shows what emptiness there is in the whole of this scheme of sensual gratification. "All that is in the world, the lust of the flesh, the lust of the eyes and the pride of life," comes everywhere at last to the same result, and to the same confession, "Vanity of vanities, all is vanity."

Second, Behold the bitter disappointment. The grand entrance to the banquet hall is opened. Every eye is directed to it. The whole multitude rise to look with eagerness and anticipation of delight. But no queen of beauty appears. The seven royal chamberlains return, mortified, humbled, trembling. Their fears might well be great. The likelihood of the result was instant death to them. The rage of the drunken king would know no bounds, and be satisfied with no explanation. Should he issue the command for their instant death, it would be at once obeyed. The breathless multitude wait to hear the explanation. The chamberlains approach the royal seat and give this answer to their message: "Queen Vashti refused to come at the king's commandment by his chamberlains." Refused to come!—what a disappointment to morbid, vulgar curiosity! What a fall to intoxicated pride.

But it was a noble specimen of woman's dignity, modesty and virtue. Never was Queen

Vashti so worthy of admiration before. Beautiful as she might have been, here was displayed an ornament beyond all the glitter of outward loveliness, and all the jewels of a costly array. It was the moral beauty of a virtuous wife who refused to be degraded even by her husband, although it was her pleasure and her duty to revere his will. Lovelier far than all the external charms of the female form and features, is the purity, delicacy and dignity of the refined and elevated mind. Vashti showed herself to be a model in Persia of which a purer age and society might be proud.

But madness was in the king's heart. He was filled with an unconquerable rage. "The king was very wroth, and his anger burned in him." It was the bitterness of disappointment and mortification. A shadow of deep and immovable gloom was cast over all the joys of his festival. All his indulgence is forgotten—the happiness of his palace has passed away. The worldly heart is empty and vexed with itself. His dream of glory has vanished. Its beauty and splendor have withered completely for him.

One "dead fly" has destroyed the fragrance of the whole provision. Even the king of an hundred and twenty-seven provinces, with unlimited power of life and death, can not be supreme. Millions trembled before a man who was successfully resisted and made contemptible by a single virtuous woman. How can he endure it? What limit ought there to be to his anger or his revenge?

But is this a peculiar case in the disappointment which it describes? Was Ahasuerus the only victim of such conscious mistake in the midst of indulgence? Nay, my young friends, this is the chamber of the world. This is but the law of the house—the rule which measures out all the results. You see the madness, the disappointment, in the sensual heart, which worldly indulgence everywhere produces. Go where you will, as far as you will, still desire and imagination press further on. Something is yet demanded to complete your attainment. Deficiencies are discovered which are still to be supplied, and you reach at last the point where nothing more can be had. The message comes back in answer to your demand, filling your soul with bitterness and crowning your whole enjoyment with disappointment—" Vashti will not come at the king's commandment." Personal authority, pride of station and of will, habitual command and universal submission, unbounded wealth and power, all find at last their limit fixed. " Hitherto shalt thou come, but no further."

This is the inevitable law of the result in human pleasure. The brightest portion leaves something still to ask. The highest attainment is as unsatisfying as the lowest. Nay, far more so, indeed. The more indulged the heart may be, only the more imperious it becomes; the more accustomed to gratification, the more impatient it is of contradiction and refusal. And there comes at last a fixed point in this worldly dream, wherever or whatever it may be, where the sleeper awakes, and the blank of anguish and self-crimination alone remains. Emptiness and disappointment crown the experiment, and hide and bury all the pleasures of the past. " Vashti will not come at the king's commandment." The very object on which the thoughts and purposes had fixed themselves, completely fails. Every thing else is rejected and despised. Madness is in the heart, and the world, and all that it has and can give is hated and cursed by the disappointed soul, because its means are limited, and it fails at last to meet the full desire of an appetite that has no bounds, and of a pride which will submit to no control. This is the history of the chamber of the world. Try it as you will, and where you will, you will come to the same issue and result. Vanity, insufficiency, dissatisfaction, bitter disappointment, this is the harvest. And if you will "sow" only "to the flesh," "from the flesh" you must "reap its corruption."

Third, Behold the degradation to which this disappointment has brought its victim. The king is wretched in the presence of them all. The answer of his chamberlains is received, and there is instant silence, mournful and depressing. The crowd were ready for a shout of acclamation at the appearance of the beautiful queen. But their eager anticipations are suddenly turned into sadness and fear. The collapse is dreadful. It is a new catastrophe in Persia. The monarch, whom before they worshiped as a god, is openly despised in the presence of his people. He feels the contempt bitterly indeed. Madness is in his heart again. His inward consciousness is heavier far than the outward load. He has disgraced himself before the multitude of his people. And he feels the extremity of the degradation. What would he not give to be restored where he stood yesterday? But, ah, to restore a character lost in folly—to make others forget the dishonor we have brought upon ourelves—this is difficult indeed.

Think of this great truth, my dear young friends. Our characters, our reputation, are habitually in our own keeping. Infamy depends upon our own acceptance of it. No outward influence can finally or fatally injure the name of those who are true to God, and true to themselves. Be watchful to keep thyself pure, and God will guard thee from the malice and falsehood of others. Be really gold; be consciously upright; have no need for concealment or excuse. Acquire no reason to dread sifting or investigation; and then no slandering or persecution can injure you.

Ahasuerus is degraded, but he has degraded himself. The man who has sacrificed his virtue, his integrity, his self-respect, may be sure that, sooner or later, his sin will find him out. That which was spoken in the ear shall be proclaimed upon the house-top. "A bird of the air shall carry the voice, and that which hath wings shall tell the matter." Proper dignity in himself, the self-respect of conscious virtue, and the determined purpose to do that which was right, would have preserved the king of Persia from all this sorrowful and mortifying result.

But this is another lesson in the chamber of worldly indulgence. This is the habitual end of a life of mere sensual gratification. Personal degradation is its habitual result—in some shape or other, its final, inevitable result. Moral, outward degradation, frequently! Instances of this crowd our land and fill our cities. Young men who began life respected and promising, whom the indulgence of unlicensed and destructive appetite has brought to the lowest condition of moral pollution and disgrace; young women, whose dawn was innocence and purity, and whose evening is the grave of lust, and the hidden debasement of conscious ruin and public abhorrence. The path is an open and a beaten one. Unrestrained desire, calling for unlimited gratifications, leading to inevitable crime, bringing its victims to social dishonor and abhorrence —this is the rule in the line of sensual enjoyment. Nothing else can bring on man outward and relative disgrace; not poverty—that may be honorable; not deformity, not disease, not persecution—all these may create increased sympathy and reverence. But sin, crime, moral delinquency, depraved appetites indulged habitually, always in the end entail degradation and social abhorrence upon their victims and votaries.

Intellectual, conscious degradation, social degradation! what can be more degrading than such a subjection? Ah, see, who is that victim of insanity, every hour pacing the floor of his asylum, measuring out his distances, wheeling and firing in melancholy repetition? Said his eminent father, "He that seeks for revenge in a duel, let him first go and see my poor son." Who is that loathsome victim of intemperance, abhorrent to the sight and smell, in filth and rags? I knew him when he spoke from the sacred desk, a professed ambassador for Christ. His station was then exalted, for his life as yet to other eyes was pure. Let any youth measure the madness filling the heart, which wine produces by its mirth, from such an example. Who was that agent of complicated and unmeasured frauds a few years since, who filled our courts with litigation and overwhelmed many a widow's heart with poverty and sorrow? I knew him when at school and in college. He was pure, lovely and excellent. But he made haste to be rich, and he could no longer be innocent. And then he fled from a society that still abhors his name, and, dying in disgrace, has left his memory dishonored, perhaps never to die.

What is there peculiar in any of these? Such instances might be multiplied by thousands, in adduced illustrations for our purpose. Thus sin ever degrades and destroys. No vail can cover it. No station can defy it. No arts can conceal it. No time can blot it out. It is leprosy within,—it will come forth. It is fire,—it will burn. It is madness in the heart,—it will speak, and mutter, and curse. And men must see and will hear. This is the chamber of the world in its sensual indulgence, and this is the law of the experiment. Ahasuerus tried it for you, in the illustration which we have before us. You see its terrible result. Why need you, why will you, try it for yourself?

What can be more degrading than such a slavery to brute appetite and sensual display? It is the defiling and destroying of a mind that might be elevated to God, and educated for glory. Begin with an observation of its downward course where you will, the current is always setting in the same direction. Follow it to the end, in whatever stream you will, the result is always the same. The victim of sensual indulgence, self-despised in every instance—openly despised by others in the most. See it in sickness, in poverty, in death. Ah, miserable are the ashes of lust. Behold it in the barren sensuality of age. Horrible is the picture which it presents. Look forward to eternity. What madness is in the heart. It burns for ever. It burns to the lowest hell. Unpardoned, rejected by a God of holiness, shunned by beings of purity, its victim lies down in sorrow and has no hope. He that was filthy is filthy still. He that was unjust is unjust still.

VII.

The Ripened Fruit of Sin.

"A furious man aboundeth in transgression."—PROVERBS, xxix. 22.

WE have still to consider this experiment of sensual indulgence in the chamber of the world. The king of Persia must teach us another solemn and painful lesson by another manifest result of his experiment. This is the abounding crime to which it leads. It begins with the grossest indulgence of appetite, and it ends in the cruelest infliction of injustice. The start is pleasure, the consummation is guilt. This is the universal rule, and we have it here exhibited in the appropriate scale and relation. We have seen the madness which is in the king's heart. We are now to see the transgression with which a furious man aboundeth.

"Vashti refused to come at the king's commandment." It is a bitter disappointment. But it can not end here. The king is excessively enraged. He has placed himself under the endurance of an open affront, a public mortification. His pride is pledged to go on to some further step of vindication. But what shall next be done? It is now a process of crime, in which every step is to further evil, and in which the king and his advisers all combined. Let us trace the sad and warning course.

First, behold the flattery and the falsehood of the world! The king is surrounded by admirers and friends. They are "wise men who knew the times;" politicians, sycophants, who always hang around the great and rich, and self-indulgent, and learn the art of meeting the demand of human pride and anger by saying the right thing at the right time for their own advancement and interest. There were seven of them in the court of Persia "who knew law and judgment, which saw the king's face, and which sat the first in the kingdom." To these seven wise men of Persia the king refers the solemn question, "What shall we do unto the Queen Vashti, according to the law, because she hath not performed the commandment of the king by the chamberlains ?"

One faithful but persecuted woman is the object of their hostility, and the subject of their counsel. But ah, where is the faithful man among them all? Why is there no one to take the side of persecuted innocence and injured virtue? What an aspect this council exhibits of the mind and motives of guilty men! How rarely do the rich and great listen to the voice of truth, or find the fidelity of real friendship! Seven princes there are, "which see the king's face and sit the first in his kingdom." But not one of them dare say to the drunken, furious monarch, " Thou art the wrong one, and Vashti is right." " Faithful are the wounds of a friend, but the kisses of an enemy are deceitful." To maintain the side of truth and virtue, against wealth and pride and power in the world, is a signal mark of a great and noble mind. But the world furnishes few such illustrations in the scenes of its indulgence and display. This is a spirit which comes from another source. A true servant of God may be even in a heathen court like Daniel, and be faithful in his earthly duty to his Master in heaven. This was Daniel to Belshazzar. Hear him: "Thou, O Belshazzar, hast not humbled thine heart, but hast lifted up thyself against the Lord of heaven; and the God in whose hand thy breath is, and whose are all thy ways, hast thou not glorified." Such was Michaiah in the court of Ahab. Hear him: "Behold, the Lord hath put a lying spirit in the mouth of all thy prophets, and the Lord hath spoken evil concerning thee; if thou return at all in peace, the Lord hath not spoken by me."

But Ahasuerus had no such friend. He shouts out the demand, "What shall we do unto the Queen Vashti?" Hear the time-serving Memucan reply to gratify his master's rage: "If it please the king, let there go a royal commandment from him, and let it be written among the laws of the Persians and the Medes, that it be not altered, that Vashti come no more before king Ahasuerus, and let the king give her royal estate to another that is better than she." Banish the faithful woman who would not pander to your vice, and to her own degradation. Sacrifice her virtue to your crime and anger. Let dignity and delicacy be made to bow down before lust and power. Ah, what an illustration is this of the kind of advice which the exalted and self-indulgent habitually receive in the world of lust and fashion! Thus hand joins in hand in the perpetration of human sin.

But does no one dissent from the ruler's cruel advice? No, no one. "The saying pleased the king and the princes, and the king did according to the word of Memucan." They all combine; united against conscience, against truth, against justice, against innocence, on the side of worldly interest and power. This is worldly wisdom, the policy of wickedness. Flattery to the king's pride and anger takes full command of the whole circle of his friends, and every virtuous and righteous principle is freely sacrificed to his will.

Is this peculiar? Was the instance solitary or unlikely? Nay, this is the chamber of the world. This is the transgression with which the world aboundeth. What swarms of flatterers hang about the path of self-indulgent youth! See that daughter of wealth and fashion. How is she led on from step to step in the blandishments of her career, under the beguilings of sycophants around, sacrificing holiness, delicacy, dignity, conscience, peace in the pursuit of the gratifications of this polluting, guilty world! How charming to her ear is the voice of the serpent! What faithful friend has she? Who is there that careth for her soul? Parents even, who should nurse this child for God, can combine in this fearful offering of all the interests of her eternity upon the shrine of mere sensual pleasure. There is none to restrain, none to warn, and she has no real friend to whom she can be induced to listen. Her steps press on in the path of disappointment and sin, like a bird to the snare of the fowler.

See that dissolute and self-indulgent young man! What degraded sycophants, bloodsuckers, hang around him, ready to second all his crimes, and to applaud the madness of his folly! As long as he has youth and wealth to waste in the bacchanals of sensual mirth, so long will he find

THE RIPENED FRUIT OF SIN. 119

companions who will sing with him the drunkard's song, and applaud his obscenities and his riot. But has he no friend? No. His own friend, and his father's friend, he has long forsaken. There is no voice of warning or wisdom to which he will listen. He is driven headlong onward, "like an ox to the slaughter, or like a fool to the correction of the stocks."

This is the chamber of the world. This is the law and habit of its sensual indulgence. If there be found an element which is an exception to this rule, it is from some other principle and source. It is not of the world itself. The scheme of sinful men is to add iniquity unto iniquity, and to encourage each other in their course of selfishness and guilt. The breath of flattery fanning the rage and revenge of Ahasuerus to still further crime, is but a type and specimen of what this sinful world everywhere exhibits. Memucans abound wherever appetite asks an excuse for the gratification it seeks.

Second. See the total want of domestic confidence, the violation of that pure and mutual family dependence which follows in the train of earthly selfishness and sensuality. What a reason this prince of the kingdom of Persia gives for his cruel and unjust advice! "This deed of the queen shall come abroad unto all women, so that they shall despise their husbands in their eyes, when it shall be reported, the king, Ahasuerus, commanded Vashti, the queen, to be brought in before him; but she came not. Likewise shall the ladies of Persia say this day unto all the king's princes who have heard of the deed of the queen. Thus shall there arise too much contempt and wrath. And when the king's decree, which he shall make, shall be published throughout all his empire, all the wives shall give to their husbands honor, both small and great." What a motive is this! Memucan's grand fear alleged is, that all the wives in Persia will prove either too virtuous to be degraded, or too rebellious to be governed.

Nothing marks a debased and consciously criminal mind more clearly and habitually than its suspicion and incredulity of the virtue and integrity of others. Why did a great statesman in England profess to govern on the principle "that every man has his price," but that his own debased mind and conscience compelled him thus to acknowledge of himself? This habit of judging others by ourselves is an old proverb among men, and it is this habit which really perpetuates the dominion and power of crime. It makes a calculation upon iniquity, an atmosphere for sin, a seed of evil doers. This absence of mutual confidence among men, this calculation upon the actings of human sin, is the source of most of the power which sin has among men to propagate itself.

You will see this in public, when bribery and deception of every kind are employed by men of corrupt and debased minds to accomplish their own selfish and ambitious ends. You will find it equally in domestic life, when the consciousness of personal guilt destroys the reverence for virtue and piety, and annihilates the repose and trust with which the members of a household should be able to confide in each other.

This painful and disgraceful fact is brought before us in our present illustration. It is the family relation of which Memucan speaks.

What is it that maintains in our households the spirit and dominion of mutual confidence? What is it that unites all the hearts in a happy, truthful home, in mutual dependence and love? I answer, not the world or the pursuit of the world, but the power of true religion, the fear and the love of God, the consciousness of a heart that really tries to do his will, and confides in the assurance that he will protect and guide others in the same blessed path. Take this great principle of life and truth from the household, let the world rule there in its pride of covetousness, or in its lust of indulgence, and how soon, and how thoroughly are domestic happiness, dignity and peace sacrificed and cast away! Mutual suspicion, recrimination, alienation, separation, divorce, hatred, persecution, murder, all follow in the legitimate train of succession as natural and too often habitual results. A member of a rich household, composed of parents and adult children, once said to me, "Sir, our house is a perfect hell." The lust of wealth, and the scramble for its partition left no filial or fraternal love and confidence behind. How often have I seen the same sad scene repeated! How often have I beheld the struggles in the division of an inheritance, the contest for individual supremacy, and the indulgence of a growing bitterness of unreasonable temper, alienating for life members of a household, that else "like kindred drops had mingled into one."

This corrosive principle of domestic sorrow and death may vary in its shape. As it is seen on a larger or more public scale among men, it may vary in its extent of field and its objects for contention. But it is always found in the chamber of the world. It is native to the corrupt and guilty heart of fallen man. "From whence come wars and fightings among you? Come they not hence? even of your lusts that war in your members? Ye lust and have not; ye kill and desire to have, and can not obtain; ye fight and war, yet ye have not, because ye ask not. Ye adulterers and adulteresses, know ye not that the friendship of the world is enmity with God! Whosoever, therefore, will be the friend of the world is the enemy of God. Do ye think that the Scripture saith in vain, the spirit that dwelleth in us lusteth to envy." (James, iv.)

Thus the apostle admonished in his day, and his admonition is equally true in ours. "No peace to the wicked," is the doom of man in every relation in which he stands. He feels this in his relations to his fellow-men. Half the talent and ingenuity of the world is exercised in plans for counterworking and overreaching the schemes of other people, or in self-defense against their violence or fraud. What an exhibition this makes of human sin! What a history of the transgression in which a furious man aboundeth! The children of the world expend their life and time and powers in suspecting, watching, guarding, forestalling each other. This is the great craft of man, personal, social, political. Is it not so? But what an acknowledgment this is of the actual influence and result of earthly appetite, and earthly indulgence? What a confession of the guilt, and of the mutual hostility of sinful men!

And where is the cure for all this? Certainly nowhere but in the influence and power of the gospel, and in the dominion and new creation of the Saviour and the Holy Spirit. The hearts of men must be converted and renewed. The souls of men must be reconciled to God, and be at peace with him, before they will abolish their mutual hostility and suspicion, and be at peace with each other. But such a change will not be found in the chamber of the world. This may teach us its necessity, but can furnish no illustration of the nature of its supply. For this manifestation of divine power we must pass into another chamber of instruction under the providence of God, which we will visit by and by.

Third, see the actual crime to which this course of indulgence in sensuality must lead. The king assents at once to the cruel and unjust advice which he receives. "The saying pleased the king and princes, and the king did according to the word of Memucan." The queen is banished and disgraced though she has done no wrong, and suffers by the hostility of man, for virtue's sake. The self-indulgent monarch finds himself involved in the grievous injustice and wrong which has been the result of his own sin.

"The furious man aboundeth in transgression." "Lust when it is conceived, bringeth forth sin; and sin, when it is finished, bringeth forth death."

This is the regular process through which the worldly and the ungodly habitually travel. I do not mean to say that they are all allowed to attain this result of open crime. The providence of a gracious God often interposes to keep men back from the results of their own choice. Merciful indeed is this interposition. Who can tell to what an extent of wickedness a rebellious world would run, but for the interference of this unseen divine restraint? But such a restraint is a special and peculiar interposition in the case of individuals. The rule is the universal product and dominion of crime, as the result of a worldly choice and sensual indulgence. Often indeed the victim is hurried onward to a terrific and unexpected fall, where all that has been pure, lovely and of good report, like the shield of Saul is vilely cast away; where the youth of comparative innocence is buried in all the horror and defilement of extreme degradation, an outcast from men. Such cases are not the exceptions in human history. They are the rule, the regular working out of the principle of atheistic and selfish depravity; and men are compelled to acknowledge the fact of this native and unceasing tendency in sin to disgrace and ruin.

When intemperance sinks into poverty and rejection,—when fraud and robbery bring the victim to a felon's cell,—when vanity and indecorous exposure prove the destruction of female virtue,—when anger and revenge result in bloodshed and murder—men are not astonished. They recognize in all these the natural issues of the principles we have traced. The instruction we here get in the chamber of the world is designed to show us this connection. Whosoever tries the experiment in our sight, tries it for us, that we may see it and shun it for ourselves. The child of self-indulgence is crime. Ahasuerus proves it, and we see the result. Multitudes besides have proved it on different scales of self-gratification, with the same results. And as we are permitted to witness the ever-repeated scene, the admonition comes to us, "Enter not into the path of the wicked, and go not in the way of evil men; avoid it; pass not by it; turn from it and pass away."

Fourth. See how surely the day of regret must come to human guilt. The king has finished his purpose and the advice of his attendants. But he is far from peace. Sin can never satisfy the sinner. "After these things, when the wrath of King Ahasuerus was appeased, he remembered Vashti, and what she had done, and what was decreed against her." This day of gloomy retrospection surely follows upon the day of mad indulgence. Human wrath can not last for ever. The whirl of the excitement passes, and then comes the bitterness of the memory of sin. The outward noise of the provocation is silenced, and the inward voice of conscience speaks. The day of pleasure has departed, and the night of reflection succeeds to it.

The soul is filled with remorse—literally, a biting, gnawing of itself. It is the fearful result of human sin. With what horror the murderer surveys his pale and bleeding victim, and longs to see some sign of life and possible restoration still remaining. Ah, what would he not give could he rebuild again the tabernacle his mad revenge has overthrown! With what bitterness of hatred or dismay the adulterer beholds the ruin of the vain child who throws herself upon his promise and his power, while dishonor and degradation hang over them both a black and gloomy cloud! What would they not do could they restore the dominion of the virtue lost, and regain the atmosphere of forfeited respect!

This is the chamber of the world. In all these, in all such cases, there comes the question that will be answered, "What fruit had ye then of those things whereof ye are now ashamed? for the end of these things is death." This is ever the result. What remembered follies crowd upon the mind! What neglected duties rise up again to view! What murdered victims cross the field of involuntary vision! The sinner looks back upon life with shame and unappeasable regret. This is inevitable. It will habitually come to him in the present life.

And even if it can be charmed or driven away through this life, come it must and come it will, only the more fearful and bitter for the delay. The postponement of the hour of remorse will but increase its intensity of woe. The silent hour of sickness, of sorrow, of poverty, of solitude, of death, of eternity, has then assumed the reign. Outward things are all forgotten. The soul looks inward and holds communion with itself. A thousand Vashtis are remembered, what they have done and what they have suffered. It is a deeply convincing hour. New and wonderful light is poured in upon the conscience. Memory is quickened and enlarged with amazing energy and minuteness. The things past can not be forgotten. Man possesses the sins of his youth. The iniquity of his heels compasses him about. A thousand thoughts and acts long forgotten repossess the soul. Filial ingratitude, domestic injustice, social fraud, sensual pollution, vicious appetite, criminal degradation, religion despised, Sabbaths profaned, resolutions broken, warnings rejected, opportunities of salvation neglected and lost!

Ah, what specters are these to assault and haunt the crowded brain! What retrospects of a privileged but miserable past! What prospects of an hopeless and more miserable future! And this is the end of self-indulgence. This is its sure result. Such reward have all they who despise the divine counsels and grieve and quench the Holy Spirit. This have they at the hands of the Lord, that they lie down in sorrow, and lift up their eyes in torment. It is a sorrow which hath no end. It is a torment, the smoke of which ascendeth up for ever and ever.

This is the end of the sensual indulgence of the world. This is the teaching of the divine providence, as we study it in this chamber of the world. This is all of earth and of earthly lusts. Its best is vanity. Its habitual course is disappointment and degradation. Its legitimate, uniform result is crime. Its final fruit is the bitterness of everlasting remorse. What a lesson is this! How distinctly and solemnly this picture of Ahasuerus teaches it to us!

Is not this lesson truth? Is not its application universal? Do we not all see it and read it, over and over again, in every scene of worldly things? Your own experiments may be upon a far smaller scale, and in a far narrower field; but the principles, the history, the distinguishing facts, the final results of this experiment, will be the same. Well may you survey the scene with aversion and dismay, with anxious desire to escape from the assembly and to renounce the secrets of the ungodly; well may you seek instead that glorious kingdom which God hath offered to you in his own dear Son—a kingdom which can not be removed, and in which nothing entereth to defile, or to perish, for ever.

Ah, seek that kingdom, my dear young friends. Seek it in Jesus, an atoning, pardoning, ruling Saviour. Seek it faithfully under the teaching and guidance of his own offered Spirit. Seek it earnestly, with your whole heart, in affectionate, effectual prayer. Seek it constantly through your whole life as the great end of your being, the glory and happiness of your best and your immortal nature. Seek it at a Saviour's feet with true repentance, truly confessing your sins. Seek it with a steadfast, trusting faith, never doubting the sure readiness of the Lord to hear and bless you. Seek it with hopeful joy, for no one who truly seeks shall fail to find. There will you meet with no disappointment, and mourn over no deficiency of supply. "Follow the Lamb whithersoever he goeth, and the Lamb which is in the midst of the throne shall feed you, and shall lead you to living fountains of waters, and God shall wipe away all tears from your eyes."

VIII.

The Short-Lived Treasure.

"The fashion of this world passeth away."—1 Corinthians, vii. 31.

THE apostle speaks of the world as if it were a pageant which has been exhibited and is over; a procession which is on the march and has passed by; a scene picture which drops for a moment and then gives way to another which succeeds it. The KOSMOS, this present arrangement of outward, visible things, which God has so mercifully contrived for man's temporary abode, and the provisions and joys of which man transforms into continued instruments and occasions of sin, is in an unceasing process of change. As its various parts, and the successive displays of divine Providence in them, accomplish their appointed results, new scenes and new agents take their place. Here there is no continuing city for man. If he would have a kingdom which can not be removed, he must seek it beyond the limits of the present world, among the things which are unseen and eternal.

The views which we have now taken of the world, in the utmost glory of its indulgences, have singularly confirmed this truth. We have seen its rapid passage, the manner of its passing, and the results which it produced. We are now to proceed to the second chamber of instruction, opened for us in this school of providence. But before we enter there let us linger for a moment as in the hall between and look back upon the affecting scene which has gone by. We have contemplated a remarkable exhibition, and it must not be passed over hastily, or be easily forgotten. We have seen the fashion of the world displayed on a large scale, and with many distinct and important results, and we may well stop for a moment and think of what we have seen.

Our first reflection must be that of our present text. It passeth away. It has gone. All its indulgences and all its glories have come to their appointed end. Nothing of them remains. We stand and look back upon the place where

Ahasuerus feasted and Vashti suffered. All is silent and dead. No single voice of the glory or of the sorrow remains. We may go our distant voyage to the river Ulai, on the banks of which this pageant passed; the works of God abide; the placid stream still flows; the lily still grows upon its banks; the sun sees his image in its waters by day, and the stars behold each other mirrored there by night. But where is the splendor of Shushan and the gorgeous palaces which adorned its banks? Not one stone remains upon another of all the palaces of its glory, or the portals of its majestic display. All have gone. Desolation and a wilderness occupy the place. Wild beasts of the desert abide there.

How wonderfully contrasted are the works of God and the works of man! The one has perished. The others remain. Of all the glory of human architecture and wealth which astonished generations looked upon there, nothing remains. A wilderness spreads itself out, over which the Arab drives his foaming steed and in which no civilized inhabitant dares to dwell. The mingled scene of splendor and iniquity which we have seen transacted in Shushan passed rapidly by. Wealth and indulgence, power and display were equally short-lived and worthless. All faded away like a dream of the night. The very form of their magnificence is lost to be recovered no more.

But is not this equally true of earth in all the relations and displays of its glory? Look where you will, you see the same history continually repeated. The bloom of youth, the gayety of health, the boast of riches, the clarion sound of triumph and power, all, all, pass away. They live a moment; they shine for a day; and they are gone. Man tries in vain to prolong their enjoyment and their being; or even to recover their shape, and perpetuate their memory. He is doomed to disappointment in them all. The retrospect is sadness and self-condemnation.

Ah, how often have we followed this noisy but sorrowful procession! We can recall hundreds of instances in our own observation, even before old age has come upon us, of the actual being of all that seemed desirable on earth, completely perished, gone forever. Even in the places which knew them, they are remembered no more. Our present scriptural subject is but one out of a multitude, in principle and experience all alike.

As we stand in the interval between the two great lessons of providence which we are to study, we may well assume the full result of the first. There at least we may say, My heart and my hope shall not be fixed. Something better than this I must have and will have. The joys that fade so rapidly and so certainly, are not for me. To be always at sea, tossed with tempests and not comforted, shall never be my chosen portion; still less to be shipwrecked upon a coast so cheerless and so barren. This world, and all the things which are in this world, shall never be the treasure of my choice.

As our second reflection upon this accomplished scene, the manner of its passing has been most remarkable. In the lesson we have considered, God has been pleased to show us this experiment on the grandest scale. The world began with every possible advantage for its working and its display, and in every succeeding step it went downward until it came to nothing. Its first scene was its brightest one. The morning rose when the tide was at its full, and the surface calm as the molten silver. Every hour marked its rapid ebb, till the evening closed upon a full accumulation of defilement and disgust, which the preceding show had vainly covered for a season. All that could be had, was had in the beginning; all that was hopeful in the future was out of its possession, and beyond its reach. It was a sad experiment indeed.

Yet I should be unwilling, my young friends, to trust you with the offer of such an experiment for yourselves. The attractions of present appetite and self-indulgence are too overpowering to the youthful heart to be allowed an opportunity of unlimited gratification. In the principles of this experiment, you remember, there was nothing peculiar. In the manner of its passage and trial it was a universal type. In all our possessions of the world, in the whole scheme of mere worldly enjoyment, the first is always the best. The clock of this world still strikes backward. It begins at twelve, runs rapidly round to one, and then stops. Thus its circle is complete, larger or smaller as it may happen to be.

How many have I seen, starting in all the pride of inherited wealth, closing their career in neglect and poverty. A friend of my early youth I call to mind, a merchant of great elegance of aspect, of style of living and of large commercial relations and success. His house was the admired model of taste and expenditure in the place of his abode. He was popular, influential and commanding. So he opened in appearance upon my first knowledge of his condition. His name was in everybody's mouth, as a prince and a mighty man among men. I knew him afterwards in a far distant place, in my maturity, a porter, laboring in a common store, his stately form bent with age, and his visage hardened with poverty and toil. It was an instance of wonderful reverse. But in his case, it was an instance of wonderful blessing also, for his soul found the Saviour, the friend of his poverty and his age, whom it had neglected as unknown, in the days of his wealth and earthly splendor.

How many have I beheld the center of personal admiration in the world of fashion, of earthly pomp and folly, living to be forgotten and abhorred. I knew a lady of elegance, of youthful aspect, and completely devoted to amusement and dress. Her father's wealth was large, and she was an only daughter. His vanity lavished upon her every joy and jewel that she desired. She flourished in a southern city during the years of her youth and early womanhood, and made our northern watering places sound with her annual display. Her appetite for excitement, however, burst all the limits of possible earthly gratification. Her whirling brain became impatient of even occasional repose. She fled to the exhilaration of opium. She attempted, with paint and dress and new extravagance, to prop up and renew her daily fading beauty. Alas, all was vain! Her family, her husband, her connections, were all made a sacrifice to her lust for this destroying agency. I was called to visit her in her last and lonely days, when she was dying in poverty. Rags were her clothing and her bed; and though, perhaps, not more than forty years of age, her form was doubled with premature decay, haggard with the embers of the secret fire which had consumed her, and so disgusting and loathsome by the destroying power of opium, that, though I had been familiar with her career and intimate in her family, it was almost impossible to recall her appearance in a connected imagination. Yet this was the sensual indulgence of the world as it had passed. I would that I could say, as in the former instance, she had found a Saviour in her wretchedness. Alas, her drunken and crazed mind allowed no such blessing. Literally, the only vessel that stood beside her in that horrid chamber, was a broken stone jug, in which she had somehow obtained her last supply of laudanum. And she died in the darkness of an intellect that had been completely overthrown by its power.

These are sad illustrations; but others, not unlike them, crowd upon my memory. Many such have I seen, dispensing pleasure to hundreds of retainers in different scenes and measures of the world, sunken at last, as the victims of disease and wretchedness, neglected and unknown, forgotten in the land of the living even while yet alive. Thus this present world repays its votaries. And when the result comes in age, or sickness, or poverty, or neglect, and the whole machine has run down and stopped, bitter and disgusting indeed is the remembrance of the world which has gone. The disappointed spirit curses the memory and the agents of its folly and its destruction; imputes the blame to any or all who have been connected with its sin; but can not, will not, come down to the actual acknowledgment of its own guilt, or justify God who has thus allowed it to reap the fruit of its own sowing.

This is the passage of this worldly pageant. You may stand in this hall of separation and see and say all this. Yes, the first of earth is always the best it has to offer, and it is only while all its adjuncts can be combined, that it is any thing, or can do any thing, for man's enjoyment or advantage.

But what a contrast there is between this passing worldly portion and the reality of that treasure which stands in opposition to it! The heavenly portion ever grows more and more compensating and satisfactory. The heart never grows old or dull in the faithful pursuit of it. The spirit which loves and seeks the things above, is always young and always fresh. Each day, each year, makes Jesus more precious, his service more attractive and his promises more blessed and compensating to man. The things below are a fading treasure. The things above are incorruptible, undefiled, unfading for ever. There, there alone, can our treasure be safely laid up. O, let us seek it and keep it there.

Third. In this passage of the world you may see what are the elements of its short-lived power to please—what are the facts which make up the necessity of this rapid rush of all that sinful man has sought and desired on the earth. Ahasuerus had every thing which a mere sensual mind could ask. Why could he not be satisfied? What formed the necessity of his wretchedness in the midst of it all?

We may answer at once, because nothing of all that he had, was adapted in itself to give him satisfaction. This is the first difficulty. There is no real proportion between the wants of man, and the things of earth alone. You have a spiritual nature, a soul within which can never be satisfied with the mere shams of an earthly life. Get what you may of them, there is still an inward want, which nothing visible or temporal can ever fill. The soul looks out in the midst of all the joys of earth unmet and unhappy, unable to be contented thus, because there is no real proportion between the two. There is here an original and inseparable defect in the things of the world, which no multiplication of them can supply.

These joys and treasures are all short-lived and perishing in themselves. They are but the fading raptures of an evening's whirl, the pleasures of an excited hour, the passing glory of a summer's season. In themselves they perish. They have the sentence of death within themselves; and you can not prolong the period of their power. They corrupt and decay in your hands while you grasp them. And you live on with new and ever-enlarging desires while they are perishing as you behold them. They are but grass, and the flower of the grass—green in the morning, withered in the evening. The word of the Lord alone endureth for ever.

The appetites which desire and seek these joys pass away with them also. There soon comes the time when there is no longer a susceptibility to their power. Their invitations find no longer a response in the heart to which they are offered. The voices of singing men and singing women can be heard no more. The attractions of earthly giddiness have become repulsive. The taste for them is lost. And this with no reference to a change of principle or heart. No, it may be we would willingly prolong their power if we could; we would gladly renew our former gratifications in them if it were possible. But all their power to please, and all our facility to be pleased by them, have passed away and can not be recalled. The imaginations and memories may remain. But the appetites and adaptations have gone for ever.

The whole scene of which these earthly joys make up a part, also goes, and can not be arrested or recalled. Friends are gone; families are broken; homes are lost; companions have departed; the world as we knew it once was far different from the world as we know it now. We sometimes look back upon all these scenes past with the vain wish that we might in some way re-create their faded forms again; and the impossibility of this often makes a sadness which nothing can supply. The whole circle has passed its round, and we can see it no more. The fashion of the world has passed away.

We stand here to contemplate this inherent fading character in the world which has passed. What a contrast are all its provisions to the joys and advantages of real religion! The gospel of the Lord Jesus comes to us with all its precious promises and mercies. We listen and consider. Ah here are glad tidings indeed. It proclaims a Saviour. It offers free forgiveness through his blood. It begs the sinful soul to accept his mercy, and to be washed in this fountain free from every stain. It offers in him an eternal habitation of holiness, an unfading crown of life and glory. Here is perfect adaptation. Here is real substance. Here is no inherent decay. Here is no room for change of feeling or taste towards the provision which it makes for human wants. All is sufficient, all remains sufficient for ever. And while we contemplate these elements of decay and passage in the world around us, well may we turn to this glorious unchanging provision, and live for ever.

Fourth, we may look at the result of this passage of the fashion of the world. What does it leave behind? Ah, this is the worst of all. We have seen the evidence in the experiment before us. Nothing in memory. There is no remembrance of benefit or pleasure. The past gives no satisfaction. There is no room for delight in retrospection. We look back in vain for something that may gratify the memory, and delight the heart in its recall. But all is vanity. A wasted life, enfeebled powers, conscious degradation, are all the residuum of a life of sensual enjoyment in the world.

Added to this, there is extreme regret, often

the bitterness of unappeased remorse, yes, remorse. An eminent statesman of America came to his dying hour in a hotel in Philadelphia. As he lay upon his bed of anguish, lamenting in his secret mind over the folly and sin of the past, a long life of guilt, transcendent powers of mind, and loftiness of station, completely thrown away, he bid his servant bring him one of his cards. There he wrote beneath his own name in capital letters, REMORSE. He turned it over and wrote on the other side REMORSE, and laid it down. Soon his physician came in, a good and serious man. The dying man handed him the card, and asked him to read it. He read REMORSE. He bid him turn it over and read the other side. He did so, and read again REMORSE. "Yes," said the prostrate man of genius and station, "that is the whole. It is all remorse." He said no more. Yes, it is all remorse. The wastefulness of life appears; the abuse of means of benefit to others; the neglect and prostitution of our own powers of heart and mind; the throwing away of time so precious, and opportunities so valuable; the neglect of a soul that lives only to accuse and condemn; the accumulation of elements of responsibility, for the settling of which there is no provision; the gathering of a guilty life for judgment before a God who has been despised; the immovable certainty that he must condemn, and can give no hope; ah, all this is wretchedness indeed, nothing but wretchedness. The fashion of the world has passed away. Its pleasures have all departed for ever, and left us nothing but the bitter anguish of remorse.

Nothing in actual possession. What of all the array of human pleasures outlasts itself. Youth, gayety and wealth successively pass by. Man goes out of one vain indulgence into another, but carries nothing away with him. The soul is empty. He presses on in this vain succession to the end. The fact of the result remains the same. He has nothing. Pleasure has gone; time has gone; indulgence has gone; means have gone; appetites have gone; life has gone. And of the whole pageant as it has passed, nothing remains. His soul is empty. His inevitable eternity has no provision. Ah, what an accumulation for a future account. The day of reckoning remains fixed and unchangable. The record of all the past must live and revive in terrific power in that great day. All the gifts and agencies of our earthly state were designed as means of usefulness to men, and obedience to God, intended to lay up for us, in a patient continuance in well-doing, a good foundation against the time to come. We may waste them all, but they are to be met again. For them all, God will bring us into judgment. And what have we to meet that great account? Nothing of earth; nothing in ourselves; nothing in any virtues of our own. In no imaginary harmlessness or excellence of a worldly life can we stand in that great day. No, this is all emptiness. The soul is wretched; the sinner is doomed. Hope and peace have gone from him for ever. This is earth in its results.

When we survey this gloomy scene of earth, what a contrast does the gospel bring! There is a final, sufficient, glorious treasure. All that man can ask or need is laid up for him in the unsearchable riches of grace in Christ Jesus. It is a river of living water; he may drink and be refreshed for ever. It is the meat which endures unto everlasting life; the bread of heaven which giveth life to the world; whosoever feedeth upon it shall never hunger. It is pleasure for evermore, joy unspeakable and full of glory; durable riches and righteousness; a treasure in the heavens which faileth not. Millions may possess it; millions may enjoy it. There is enough for all, and room for more, and yet of all these millions, no one shall be weary of his portion, and no inhabitant shall say, I am sick. Ah, here is substance, when shadows flee. Here is glory which abideth when fashions and pageants pass away.

My dear youth, let us make our conclusion as we stand here between the world and Christ: I will go no longer under this earthly bondage. I will now try another and better system. I will say unto that Holy Spirit who is the great teacher of the soul, lead me into the chamber of true religion, let me hear of that, let me embrace it, and enjoy it. With another hope, and with another view, I will press on to the glory that excelleth. I shall surely find in Christ a full and living Saviour for my soul, that which I can find nowhere else beside. I long, I am determined, to count all other things but loss that I may win Christ. In him is life. Let that life be mine for ever.

IX.

The Weak and Lowly.

"God hath chosen the weak things of the world to confound the things which are mighty."—1 Corinthians, i. 27.

This is one of the great lessons of the divine Providence. It is also one of the special lessons for which the story of the Captive Orphan is given to us. The first of these four lessons we have well considered, and I trust have derived profitable and important instructions from it. We come now to take up the second. We enter the chamber of true religion. We are to contemplate the secure prosperity of real piety, the certainty of their happiness and success whom God has chosen and who love God. It is a most precious lesson, and one illustrated in the whole history of the Lord's family. Who that has loved and trusted him was ever confounded? When was the righteous ever forsaken? or how can they be harmed who are followers of that which is good?

Poor, helpless, feeble, may be the earthward aspect of true religion. But the great principle of our text is always true and always demonstrated. God chooses "the weak things of the world to confound the things which are mighty, and base things of the world and things which are despised hath God chosen—yea, and things which are not, to bring to naught things that are."

In the management of this new subject of the divine Providence we see the same governing rule as in the former illustration. It is the universal rule of God's righteous government. He will manifest his power and his truth, by giving every possible advantage to the side which opposes him. He will allow his enemies to have the utmost combination of strength on their side, in order that he may show them how easily he can scatter them, as the chaff before the wind, that no flesh may glory in his presence. When we come into this second chamber of instruction, every aspect of the cause which is to triumph is seen to be reduced and brought low. Beggars shall be taken from the dunghill, to set them among princes. God will be indebted to no outward help or influence. He will make the contrast perfect and entire. This we shall see remarkably illustrated in the case which is presented to our contemplation. The prospect as it opens is discouraging in an extreme degree. But the end is exalted and glorious, just as in the former illustration, the end was wretched and ruinous, while the outset was grand and promising.

It is a new picture which we have before us, beautiful in itself, striking in its arrangements, deeply affecting in its details, wonderfully triumphant in its results. This is the CAPTIVE ORPHAN of ISRAEL, whose personal history now comes out to view.

As we enter upon this new scene we see how God is pleased to overrule the very sins and passions of guilty men for the accomplishment of his own designs. The banishment of Vashti has left Ahasuerus solitary and self-reproaching. Some scheme must be adopted by those who counselled her overthrow, to supply her place. "Then said the king's servants that ministered unto him, let there be fair young virgins sought for the king." Their purpose was the mere gratification of the monarch's appetite and taste. But God's design was to exalt his chosen, and to make even the sins of men to praise him. "Let the king appoint officers in all the provinces of his kingdom that they may gather together all the fair young virgins unto Shushan, the palace. And let the maiden that pleaseth the king be queen instead of Vashti. And the thing pleased the king and he did so."

How perfectly natural was all this arrangement and plan! And yet it was but one part of God's divine arrangement to bring about his own plan, a plan of which they knew nothing. Thus he leaves men to act out their own purposes, and accomplish their own ends, and yet overrules their whole scheme for the attainment of the results which he has already determined. This is his providence; this is the wise and perfect government of the Most High. And as we pass on to survey the new scene which opens to us, this is our introduction to its attractive and remarkable features and events.

As the door opens for us to our new lesson, the simple history which introduces it is as follows: "Now, in Shushan, the palace, there was a certain Jew whose name was Mordecai." He was the descendant of one who had been carried away captive out of Judea, when Ezekiel had his early vision, and Daniel testified for the Lord in the court of Nebuchadnezzar. When other families of Israel returned to their own land by the permission of Cyrus, the family of Mordecai remained in the land of their captivity. "And he had brought up Hadassah, that is Esther, his uncle's daughter, for she had neither father nor mother, and the maid was fair and beautiful; whom Mordecai, when her father and mother were dead, took for his own daughter." This is the attractive and interesting object in our view. Let us stop for a moment to contemplate her character and condition as she now appears.

First, we see a youthful female, a poor girl. Her very sex betokens weakness and exposure.

The female sex is called in the Scripture "the weaker vessel." Not from mental inferiority, not from moral depression or deficiency, not from poverty of social influence, not from justifiable degradation in social relations. No, in all these things woman is, and is designed to be the equal and companion of man. Nay, more; in her very relations to him by nature, she is the instructress of his youth, the preserver and guardian of his early being and character, the example and model to which his plastic infancy becomes conformed. Nothing more displays a low and savage state of man, individual or social, than his treating the female sex with contempt, or impudence, or cruelty, or sensuality, as if woman were made merely to be the victim of his passion, or the butt of his reproaches. Be assured, my young friends, a reverence for that sex, for its purity, its delicacy, its propriety, its dignity, its holiness, eminently becomes and distinguishes a refined and cultivated mind and people. As Christian influence enlarges its adorning and renewing power in society, and the gospel of the Lord Jesus becomes more perfectly the rule of life and manners among men, the acknowledgment and the cultivation of this great principle and habit of social life will distinguish human society more and more.

But yet woman is called "the weaker vessel," and is so, as the crystal vase is a weaker vessel than the oaken cask, more easily overthrown, more surely injured, more irreparably destroyed, by the power of vicious habit, or sinful temptation. To her, exposure to evil is far the heavier, and far more dangerous. Upon her, sorrows press with a far more grievous load. To her, misfortunes come with a far more sharpened power. For her, recovery from moral and social degradation is far more difficult; and to her, oppression and hostility are far more dreadful and resistless.

The wrongs of women have filled every age, and every history. No age, no people seems yet to have reached the ground where woman is made equal to man in social advantage, and is not beyond him in social distress. Does poverty come upon a family? Does death desolate an habitation, or remove a father from his household? Our first question is, Is there a widow, are there daughters there? and if we can be answered in the negative, we breathe more freely at once. The case is easier to relieve, a remedy for the sorrow is far more readily found. How long this shall be we can not tell. That it shall not be always, we surely believe.

We often hear that the gospel has brought great privileges and relief to the female sex, and so far as the gracious principles and commands of the gospel are concerned, it is entirely true. So far as the just influence of the gospel is actually carried out, so far also is it really true in fact. The Saviour came as the seed of woman. He found his faithful and cherished friends among women. He ministered to their healing and salvation and social comfort with assiduity and delight. He welcomed them as companions of his journeys. He loved them as the grateful ministers of hospitality and kindness to his wants. He blessed them for their sympathy in his hours of sorrow. He forgot not their widowed loneliness and sorrow in the moment of his departure. The dignity which his personal ministrations appended to the sex, the teachings of his gospel are designed to perpetuate. But this gospel wars with so much that is ungodly and selfish and sensual on earth, that the victory for woman is like the other victories to be obtained by its power, clogged with unceasing hostility, and impeded by the abiding wickedness of a world in sin, and the blessedness of its full results among the human race is still the subject of prophetic anticipation and hope.

But here when the illustration of rising, conquering piety is brought before us, the subject is a woman; and a woman in her weakest and most forlorn position, a lonely girl; Ah, let us bless God that his eye is never shut that it can not see, nor his ear heavy that it can not hear. It is enough for us to see and know that God is there, the Father of the fatherless, and the God of the widows in his holy habitation. All things are naked and open to him. But the defenseless condition of this daughter of Israel presents the special interest of the history before us. If the experiment had been with man, not half our fears would have been awakened, nor half our interest have been excited.

Second, she is an orphan girl. "She has neither father nor mother." This is enough. What a pang it seems to give at the very outset. An orphan is a title sorrowful and depressing enough in any condition and in either sex. If we concede to it wealth and outward comforts, these are much. They alleviate much of the outward distress, and are instruments of defense against many of the outward evils of the condition. But they do not touch the great point of the sorrow. Can they bring them back again? Father and mother gone, make the world, to the ingenuous and affectionate youth, a tasteless or a bitter thing.

My young friends, what a privilege are parents spared to bless and cheer our maturity! What a joy and cause for thanksgiving is it to be permitted even to shelter and cheer their age in our own home! Few privileges in life are greater. And the presence of an aged parent, whatever care may attend it, is always a blessing to one, who with a truly grateful heart desires to do the will of God.

When the eminent Richard Cecil was born, he was the child of his mother's old age, and her heart was overwhelmed with sorrowful anticipations connected with his birth. Yet we read of her afterwards as living to find him the peculiar joy and solace of her declining years. What a privilege is such a son! And how great to him was the blessing of being able to recompense his mother's toil, and to comfort and honor the years of her age! I pray you all to value this privilege, and to make it the effort of your life to bring it into complete effect in your own experience of such a relation.

But far earlier than this possible result, how great, in the period of your youth, is the privilege of a happy parental home! How great the blessing of growing up amidst the combined objects and sources of affection! Ah, be thankful for such a privilege, if it is yours. Improve it to the uttermost. Adorn it with watchful effort. Recompense it with an humbly cheerful, happy obedience. It is a blessed gift to you, and when once lost, is never to be renewed on earth.

What solitude, separation, want of confidence, fear, distrust, yea, often anguish, often fill up the orphan's heart. Few can sympathize; and even to those few, it is impossible to pour out the secret sorrows which are the burden and distress within. Many of the orphan's sufferings may be treated as unfounded. The sensitive spirit may be much tempted to imagine neglects intended, where none were designed, and cruelties inflicted, where only absence of mind or irritable forgetfulness had intervened in the feelings of others. But imaginary as the causes may be, the sorrows which they produce are real and abiding. And they claim a peculiar degree and a peculiar manifestation of consideration and kindness from surrounding friends.

Yet, when we add poverty to the orphan's lot, what increased bitterness do we throw into the cup! Many a dying mother has looked upon the infant child whom she was leaving, the living monument of her sorrow, with the heartfelt wish that she could have seen the babe go before her. And yet even then, when the child is left for other hands to nurture, and for other hearts to love, how much in the apparent prospect depends upon the sex. An orphan boy may struggle. The very poverty which oppresses him may excite his energies and call out his powers of endurance and of action. His self-dependence is aroused. His industry and enterprise are called into the field. He may be made by his very loneliness to aspire to much, and to accomplish much, that in luxury he would never have thought of, or if he did, have attempted to gain.

But an orphan girl in poverty! what human case is habitually harder? Every thing in her sex, and every thing in her condition, is against her. Her exposure to the wickedness and the arts of the corrupt, is the subject of constant observation and of constant dread. The amount of human wretchedness gathered from this one sad field of experience, is enormous, and witnessed every day. The amount of oppression and guilt for which man must answer before God, in this relation, is terrific. What streams of vice flow down upon human society from this one source! What judgments on a community may not be expected to descend in consequence thereof! What anguish is this day filling many a heart which vice has thus crushed, and then left for misery to fix its habitation there! Hope, joy, peace, innocence, all sacrificed on the horrible altar of sensual debasement. And to all this, the loneliness of female orphanage too often and too sadly exposes.

But here in the case of a female orphan is the commencement of our exhibition of the security and triumph of true piety in this second experiment. We are far from having fully considered the difficulties and dangers which must threaten it. But we must stop here. We shall see that the Redeemer of the fatherless is mighty; that God in his holy habitation is able to protect. Over such he proclaims his special paternal care. When their father and their mother forsake them, then the Lord taketh them up. And in the manifestation of his power to bless, to comfort and to save, he will begin his display of the course and triumph of true piety, in loneliness and destitution like this.

I will adduce no other elements of the captive's condition at present. I shall rejoice to fix in your heart and memory some great principles here illustrated, which I would have you never forget.

First, that God loves the lowly. He inhabiteth eternity. He sitteth on the circle of the earth, and the inhabitants thereof are as grasshoppers in his sight. Yet the man to whom he looks is the lowly one who trembles at his Word. The spirit that is self-renouncing, the condition that is consciously needy and dependent, the person who is unjustly an outcast, and for whom no man careth; these are they whom God regardeth and chooses for his own; and whose needs he abundantly supplies. "When the poor and needy seek for water and there is none, and their tongue faileth for thirst, the Lord will hear them, and the God of Israel will not forsake them." Let such put their trust in God. "He hath respect unto the lowly, but the proud he beholdeth afar off." To obtain his favor, such as these must come down, and lie low and depending before him. The spring of happiness, the beginning of prosperity is there. Learn to seek it there. Be willing to find it there. Let every imagination which exalteth itself against God be cast down. Be content to allow him to take you from the dust in all your sinfulness and unworthiness, and to wash and cleanse and save you by his own grace and power alone.

Second, forget not that your honor and happiness will always be promoted by gaining the mind of God in this relation. Look at things as he looks at them, and estimate them as he esteems them. Try to have your minds conformed to his, and your thoughts like his thoughts. This surely is the path of happiness for us. The world says, Happy are the rich, the luxurious, the self-indulgent. God says, Happy are the poor in spirit, the meek, the persecuted for righteousness' sake. Let us adopt the mind of God in this matter, and learn to regulate our views and hopes by his plans and his statements.

The weak things of the world, if he choose

them, and love them, will confound the things that are mighty. "They who trust in the Lord are like the Mount Zion, which can not be removed, but standeth fast for ever and ever." "Fear not, thou worm Jacob, I will help thee, saith the Lord. Behold, I will make thee a new sharp threshing instrument having teeth, and thou shalt thresh the mountains and beat them small, and shalt make the hills like chaff. Thou shalt fan them, and the wind shall carry them away, and the whirlwind shall scatter them; and thou shalt rejoice in the Lord, and shalt glory in the Holy One of Israel."

X.

The Beginning of True Prosperity.

"If thou wouldst seek unto the Lord betimes, and make thy supplications to the Almighty, though thy beginning was small, yet thy latter end should greatly increase."—Job, viii. 5–7.

This is the lesson which the divine Providence teaches us in the chamber of true piety. There is increasing happiness and perfect security to those who in early, faithful prayer, seek unto the Lord. When God becomes the portion of the soul, all blessings abound upon it and around it. How accurately is this stated in our text! Make your experiment of life with this simple direction. Begin to put it to the proof, and see whether God will not fulfill for you the testimony of his word.

Commence your life by seeking unto the Lord. Let the first action and offerings of your heart be in the language of affectionate supplication. Learn, under the teaching of his own Spirit, to call unto him in the earnestness of a child conscious of his father's love, "My father, thou art the guide of my youth." Let your choice of him be pure and sincere, simple and upright. Choose him as your real, your desired portion, in a practical devotion of yourself to his will and service. You will then find no doubt or question connected with his promises. He will awake and be watchful in your behalf. He will make the habitation of your righteousness prosperous. However small may be your beginning, your latter end shall greatly increase.

The Lord loves to act in such a case, and on such a principle. He takes up the poor and friendless, and those who have none to help them, and for whom no man careth. He delights to exalt them, and to set them on the thrones of kingdoms. He teaches those who are cast down to say, "When my father and my mother forsake me, then the Lord taketh me up."

This is the subject which we have now before us. Our study is in the chamber of true religion. There we see a solitary girl, and she an orphan. She hath "neither father nor mother."

On the doctrine of earthly chances, every thing is against her. But in the scheme of the divine government, we shall see that she has an Almighty Friend. Her beginning is small indeed, and disastrous enough; her latter end shall greatly increase. We will trace the circumstances of her advancing prosperity from this inauspicious commencement; first, the circumstances which are against her, the difficulties in her condition which must be overcome. Her sex and her orphan state we have already considered. But there are other discouraging circumstances also, which seem completely to forbid the latter end of advancement which is promised.

First, she is a stranger. We find her in a land not her own, though, perhaps, she was born upon its soil. Among a people with whom she has no affinity and no bond of affection. A girl, an orphan, and a stranger. Why does God so often combine the stranger and the fatherless together in his Word, but because there is such a peculiar loneliness distinguishing the condition of each? To wander among multitudes with whom we have no connection and no sympathy, is often a depression to the brightest spirits. Many an hour does even the most favored traveler find, when he feels the pressure of his solitude to a degree that it is impossible to bear in peace.

But this poor girl is not a stranger in voluntary journeying, she is a captive. She is in a land most of all incongruous with her principles and her tastes; where to be recognized is to be despised; and where her solitude and concealment may be her chief protection. She is a servant of the true God in a land of dark idolatry; a pure, praying girl amidst a people whose licentious profligacy made the most wasting crimes to be no dishonor. Poor child! As we stand in this chamber of instruction, and look upon her, we might weep over her loneliness and exposure. Well for her was the promise of her father's God to take her up. And our recovering and sustaining thought, as we contemplate her condition, is the blessed assurance that the Redeemer of the fatherless is mighty.

But if piety can be made triumphant under circumstances so completely opposed to it; and a child of God can glorify her Father's name, and keep his commandments amidst temptations and difficulties so numerous and pressing, how great will be the responsibility of those who are exposed to no such contests! What privileges attend the youthful flock to whom I speak. Look around, my dear young friends, upon your cheerful, free and happy homes, where no enemy molests you, and no oppressor's chain is felt. What blessings here crown your lives! Domestic mercies, some of God's most precious gifts, are preserved to you. The shelter of a parental home is yours. The bosom of family affection is for you. The voice of maternal kindness answers you with its delightful encouragement and welcome. A father's faithful guardianship is over you. Be not unmindful of these mercies, but be grateful for them all. Allow the action of God's tenderness and love to you to lead you to a thankful and holy dedication to his service. Let the goodness of God lead you to repentance. Remember that from them to whom much is given, much will be required. How many lonely captive orphan strangers may rise up against you in the judgment of the Lord! They sought the Lord in the day of their adversity, and they found him a very present help to them in their hour of need. But you may seek and find him now. Why should you wait for the pressure of affliction, or poverty, or lonely distress, to make you seek and love one so infinitely worthy of your heart's affections? Let this captive orphan plead with you to seek the Lord early, and guide you with gratitude and confidence to a Saviour's feet.

Second, this orphan stranger, this lonely girl, is also beautiful in person. "The maid was fair and beautiful." This is a gift which all naturally, perhaps not unreasonably, prize. It is God who hath given to the youthful form and face their attractions and their loveliness. One of the marks of his benevolence is here seen. His goodness shines in all these aspects of his power. He has made every thing beautiful in its time. He has surrounded the eye with attractive objects. Colors, forms and motions on every side, from the wings of an insect, or the gambols of a kid, or the glowing outline of the evening landscape, abound with expressions of his benevolence. Why but from this, is the world filled with objects ministering delight, rather than abounding with scenes of disgust? It is right thus to regard the evidences of his kindness; and it is but silly and affected to profess to undervalue personal beauty, or to be ungrateful for it.

Yet the beauty of our daughters is but too frequently a snare. Sin in the heart perverts and corrupts it. It is welcomed as a merchandise for gain. It is nourished as the food for vanity. It is perverted to awaken an earthly taste, and to encourage a carnal mind. It brings an attending exposure to peculiar temptations. Amidst the snares of a corrupting world, we may be often led to lament the gift, and regret, as we think of the maiden, that she is fair and beautiful. Often indeed have we cause for it while we live, and if we are to leave our youthful daughters orphans in the world, christian solicitude might lead us to lament over the beauty of a countenance which presents so manifest a temptation to sin.

Such was the snare to which this captive orphan was exposed. And as we stand and look upon her loveliness and her exposure, we are ready to say, "Poor girl, thy beauty is now but thy burden and thy danger." All the circumstances of her history combine to show her loveliness as remarkable and excelling. Her parents delighted over her childish promise, and called her Hadassah, their myrtle, their joy. They looked forward to great parental delight in her coming bloom, when as a fragrant myrtle, they should see her blossoming at their side. But this, alas, they were not to see. Their beautiful Hadassah had another path laid out for her than they would have planned in the fondness of their parental love. She was to bloom for the gaze of other eyes, but not for theirs. Her charms of person were to be an attraction to the power of licentious rapine, and not the recompense of parental watchfulness. Hazardous was the possession indeed. But Hadassah had a mighty and sufficient protector and guide. Her father and her mother must forsake her, but the Lord would take her up.

Could I lead you off from this outward beauty to think of the fair beauty of the Lord,—how much more precious and desirable is that pure and obedient mind which we find united with Hadassah's loveliness of person! That love towards God, that conformity to his image and will, the graces and ornaments which were the work of his own Spirit, the adornings which he placed upon the converted and new-created soul—how much more real and precious were these! Ah, my young friends, seek these. Outward beauty we can not all have. But this higher and more enduring beauty of the Spirit you may all possess. We are what we are towards God. In his favor, and in a temper and mind at peace with him and reconciled to him, there is a beauty which outshines all the fading attractions of the world around you. "The flower fadeth, and the beauty thereof falleth away, but the word of our God endureth for ever; and this word is that gospel which is preached unto you." Hadassah's personal outward beauty was her snare and danger; Hadassah's spiritual loveliness, her trust in God, her love for God, was her safeguard and defense. God be praised for that fair beauty which abideth in his temple for ever.

Third. The sole earthly protector of this beautiful orphan was poor and unable to defend her. "In Shushan, the palace, there was a certain Jew whose name was Mordecai. And he brought up Hadassah, that is Esther, his uncle's daughter, for she had neither father nor mother, and the maid was fair and beautiful; whom Mordecai, when her father and mother were dead, took for his own daughter." Some orphans find a new, and even a more bountiful shelter, in the habitations of the rich. But Hadassah's protector was her cousin, like herself a poor Jew, a captive in Shushan. When her father and her mother were obliged to forsake her, the Lord took her up, by providing her a faithful friend in her father's nephew. He took her for his own daughter. He sheltered and guarded her amidst the snares of Shushan, surrounded by all the tempting and destructive influences of a licentious and pagan city. He brought her up in the fear and love of the God of her fathers, amidst all the snares of surrounding sin. Whatever his employments might have been, they were but those of a poor foreigner in an unsympathizing population, and of a poor Jew in a Persian city. The crimes and sensuality of such a place were always in his sight. The arbitrary power which reigned there he had no means to resist or to avoid. He could not but daily see how different was the condition of a youthful female there, subject to be bought and sold, or seized and ravished, at the unlicensed will of wicked men of power and wealth, from the guarded and secluded condition of the maids of Israel, and the daughters of Zion, dwelling in the shelter of their mothers' tents, and beneath the wings and authority of the God of Israel. And, therefore, we can not doubt that he would use special efforts to shield and protect her, in a holy, virtuous private life, to the utmost of his power.

Hadassah was brought up under this secluded care, a sheltered Jewish maiden, watchful and timorous as the gazelle of her ancestral hills. Her new name Esther, a star, a hidden one, was

Persian, given to her probably at her discovery by the ministers of the king, to intimate her transcendent beauty, and her concealment from previous knowledge and view. Thus the day excludes the beauty of the hidden stars, and they are to be discovered and admired by those only who seek for them when their concealment passes. The king's messengers in their search for the objects to gratify the monarch's taste, drew from her concealment this hidden myrtle of Judea, and called her, in their admiration, a Persian star.

But she was really one of God's hidden ones, chosen in his love, to be protected and loved by him. He had watched over her, and for her sake had blessed the habitation of the poor. His presence had given her a divine shelter, and ordered and overruled all things for her happiness and security. Though an orphan among men, she was a child of God, and her father could never die. Under his gracious care she was kept in perfect safety. Her Redeemer was mighty, and she was happy in his defense. Blessed are they who dwell under the shadow of his wings. Never forget this highest security of his protection and his presence. There you are secure for ever. No one can be poor, who is rich in faith towards God. No one can be deserted, who has the divine friendship and fellowship. He is an everlasting friend, who sticketh closer than a brother, who in the midst of adversity never fails nor forsakes those who put their trust in him. Seek this great preserver of the poor and feeble, and in a filial loving faith in his power, make him your friend for ever.

Fourth, this lonely orphan girl was grateful and obedient. We read in the twentieth verse of the second chapter, "Esther did the commandment of Mordecai like as when she was brought up with him." This affectionate obedience to him was but the result of a higher spirit and habit of obedience to God. In the language of our present text, she sought "the Lord betimes and made her supplication to the Almighty." And God heard her prayer and blessed her with his own guidance as well as his own protection. Her humility and tender gratitude toward Mordecai were most remarkable. In every thing she obeyed him faithfully. And no influence of her unexpected and wonderful exaltation could operate to turn her heart and mind away from him, or from her grateful subjection to him. In the midst of all her power and elevation, her faithful benefactor was never forgotten or undervalued.

Happy indeed is such a manifestation of grace as this! You may build with confidence any hope of usefulness, and any desired attainment of human excellence upon a character so true. A spirit thus pure, subdued, affectionate and sincere, what may it not do that is lovely, honest, and of good report? Is there any thing more beautiful in life than this tenderness of domestic affection in a child, this grateful remembrance and acknowledgment of kindness in a youth? It spreads happiness for others around its path. It converts the cares and trials of life into pleasures and delights. It crowns the whole personal walk with loveliness and attractions. It even adorns the countenance and the person with lineaments of beauty which no art can feign, and higher than which nature can never furnish. What joy attends the education of such a mind and heart. Toil and poverty, and labor and watchfulness become the employments of delight, when endured and expended for such a child. And if an early departure takes the object of such undying affection from the sight, it is but to leave a memory behind, which is crowned with life-long blessedness, and is not corroded by a single care or regret.

But Esther's gratitude to her earthly benefactor was founded on her still deeper gratitude to God. She sought him in her youth as her own friend, and her father's friend. She carried the employments and the spirit of religion and prayer with her into the palace, and throughout her life. The fruits of her character were the manifest fruits of the Holy Spirit. She adorned the doctrine of her God and Saviour by a conversation becoming his Word and conformed to his will. This we shall see beautifully displayed. And this was the peculiar characteristic of the scene which is now before us and which makes it the object of our study.

This is the lesson which we are to learn in this second chamber of instruction. It is the very lesson of our present text. "If thou wouldst seek unto the Lord betimes and make thy supplication unto the Almighty, though thy beginning was small, yet thy latter end should greatly increase."

This poor and lonely, but faithful and beautiful girl, God means to raise up to be an eminent blessing and restorer to his people. Her latter end is to be in great prosperity. But see where she begins. Could any one be more lonely, or more reduced, or more exposed? There is every thing in the relations of earth against her. But all these obstacles are nothing with God. He means to do great things by her, and great things for her. Her latter end shall greatly increase. And when God is pleased to bless, who can hinder or oppose his will?

This is our great lesson now. We are witnessing the purpose and the work of God. He is exalting a child of his own, and showing what he can do with his own, and by his own power. No condition is beneath his notice. No child of grace is below his care. None who love him can be forsaken or destroyed. We see here a low beginning; none could be more so; but it is a very lovely one. And as we study the course through which God is pleased to lead this child of grace, we shall see him to be justified in his whole course, and to come forth completely victorious in the work which he hath undertaken.

How great is the advantage of having God upon your side, and of being under his special protection and care! "He that dwelleth in the secret place of the Most High shall abide under the shadow of the Almighty." My dear young friends, find your refuge and your place of rest in the Lord Jesus Christ, who gave himself to purchase you for God, and to purchase for you a heavenly inheritance and home with God. Live under his favour and blessing, through his Spirit. Live for him,—live with him. So shall you find a life of happiness on earth. His Spirit shall bless you. His presence shall cheer you. His providence shall protect you. You may be tossed with tempests,—you may appear to be afflicted and not comforted,—but he "will lay your stones with fair colors, and your foundations with sapphires." Your end shall be joy and peace. You "shall come to Zion, the ransomed of the Lord, with songs and everlasting joy upon your heads." "Be thou faithful unto death and he will give thee a crown of life."

XI.
The Mysterious Beginning.

"For promotion cometh neither from the east, nor from the west, nor from the south. But God is the Judge; He putteth down one, and setteth up another."—PSALM lxxv. 6.

THIS is a most important truth for us to study. Man proposes, but God disposes. The eyes of the Lord are in every place. The government of the world is on his shoulder. The soul that trusts in him is always secure, and can never be forsaken. But God gives no account to us, of his methods or plans of working to accomplish his own purposes and results. Accordingly the beginnings of his plans are often extremely mysterious and dark; clouds and darkness are round about him, and we must wait for the full issue of his great designs, before we shall see how perfectly justice and judgment are the habitation of his throne.

This is the lesson we are now studying. There is a secure and final prosperity to real love for God, and true devotion to his service. The child of God has nothing to do, but simply to honor and serve him faithfully and constantly according to his will; and all things in his condition will be ordered for his happiness and usefulness, according to the goodness of God. We have seen the lowly and lonely condition of that child of God who is brought before us here. She was a poor orphan girl, a stranger and a captive, fair and beautiful, with no other earthly protector than her cousin, a poor Jew, perhaps himself just as dependent. This faithful relative had hidden and sheltered her in his own abode, according to his power.

But the difficulties attending her adequate protection were great. The dangers and trials in her way, were many and fearful. It is very important to mark this beginning of the Lord's dealings. Every thing was accumulated, to make the path of true religion difficult and unpromising, and to show that God will be dependent on no outward circumstances of aid or advantage, in accomplishing the purposes of his love and grace. And when we now proceed to consider the history and process of Esther's exaltation, we shall find the events as they succeed each other, a remarkable illustration of the principles of our present text. It was accomplished in God's own way, and to attain the ends which God had himself designed. Whatever were the instruments or the means employed, it is still very apparent, that it was God who was putting down one, and setting up another. And the scheme which he had formed, was one of infinite love to his people, and to the child of grace, the daughter of the Lord Almighty, by whom he designed to bless them.

First, we may consider the object of this exaltation. This poor Jewish orphan is to be made the Queen of Persia. The change of position is as wide and wonderful as earth can illustrate. Why was this? Why did God thus select and elevate her!

He designed to give to all his people a great illustration of his power and goodness. He would have them see, he would have all to see how certain and adequate is his protection to those who love and trust him. He would show his independence of all human help in accomplishing the purpose which he had formed. He would thus give to ages to come the utmost encouragement to believe his Word, and to trust in him. This is a great lesson for us to learn. We are so encompassed and entangled with the things which are seen and material, that our unbelieving hearts are constantly disposed to limit God in all his plans of providence and grace to instruments of our own selection. Whatever, therefore, shall take us off from all human dependence and strength, and throw us completely upon God for our help and trust, must be an important blessing to us. It is our great gain to fix our faith on him, to learn the habit of believing him entirely, and to strive in all things to consult and to accomplish his holy will. This is the advantage of all the histories of his dealings with his people in ages past. They were written for our admonition. And as we read them we learn from the experience of all who have gone before us the great blessedness of fixing our hearts and hopes upon the Lord.

This is one great object in such an instance

of the goodness and wisdom of God. But he had further designs in this work. He not only intended to show his goodness to Esther in protecting and rewarding a child whom he loved, he also purposed to make her an eminent blessing to others. She was to be a restorer to her people, a great blessing to her own captive nation. We shall see the remarkable illustrations and proofs of this purpose in the facts of her history as we proceed. They will show both the goodness of God and the usefulness which he can confer on the most humble and lowly of his people. As Esther's history and character are developed before our view we shall find new reasons to say, "Great and marvelous are thy works, Lord God Almighty. Just and true are all thy ways, thou King of saints."

I would have you adopt from this history one general thought. No one is exalted in this world for himself alone. Whatever gifts, or gains, or influence we have, they are for the benefit of others. No man liveth for himself. Upon the life and actions of every one, many, we can never tell how many, are dependent, and are to derive thence blessings incalculable and eternal, if this life be according to the will of God. This great truth of the mutual dependence of his creatures, God illustrates for us in all the works of his wisdom and power. This is the subject of the study of the wise naturalist, to discover where he may, the proposed benefit of every divine arrangement in the world of nature. In most of the Lord's works the benefit proposed is plain enough, and apparent to our first sight. And even when it is most obscured from our perception at first, a faithful study is sure to bring it out to view. Every animal and every part of inanimate creation combines to proclaim the same fact and law of divine appointment. "No man liveth to himself."

But how clearly, and with what peculiar power does God teach us this truth in the whole plan of divine redemption. Why has the Lord Jesus lived and died? And why is he still living as a mediator at the right hand of God? "For us," is the only answer to the question. He is exalted on high that he may bestow gifts upon men. He is made the great giver, the fountain of all blessings to us, and we live through him.

This important truth God equally teaches us in our own enjoyment of the blessings which redemption brings to us. He enriches us with all our gifts, that we may be made the instruments of enriching others. Every talent and every gain is intended to be but an additional instrument of benefit to our fellow-men, and of responsibility to God. We should frequently inquire what our Father's purpose may be, in the gifts which we have received. How can they be made useful and beneficial to others? We should look around and ask, whom can I bless? Whom can I serve? To whom can I give even a cup of cold water in my Master's name?

We can never tell how wide may be the appointed influences of such a spirit. Esther could have had no idea of the purpose of her exaltation, or of the extent of benefits which God intended she should confer. The process of her preparation for this appointed result was all a mystery to her, and a very painful mystery. Many a sad and harassing thought she doubtless had in her lonely captivity in the palace, of what the God of her fathers could mean in such a strange dealing with her. Mordecai could as little understand it as she. He looked after her with sincere distress. He mourned over her with unfeigned bitterness of grief. He was ready to say like his father Jacob, "all these things are against me." "He walked every day before the court of the women's house, to know how Esther did, and what should become of her." His heart was filled with a thousand fears; and to interpret the plan, or to foresee the end, was utterly beyond his power. But we read the whole story with very different feelings. We see the end of the Lord, that he is faithful and very gracious, and we may learn from it to understand and to confide in the loving kindness of the Lord. When the gracious purpose of God comes out in the result of his dispensation, we have no longer any doubt or darkness resting upon his Word.

Second. We may consider the circumstances of Esther's exaltation. They were painful and repulsive to her in an extreme degree. Lonely and poor as was her first condition, an orphan captive child with Mordecai, it was vastly to be preferred, in her views and feelings, to the one which succeeded it. Her former sorrows were in innocence. Her new condition could hardly be anticipated in separation from sin.

She was the subject of violent compulsion. Such is the true meaning of the term "brought," literally, "brought by force." "It came to pass when the king's commandment and his decree was heard, and when many maidens were gathered together unto Shushan, the palace, that Esther was brought also unto the king's house, to the custody of Hegai, keeper of the women." She was compelled to go at the king's commandment. In this search through all the provinces for the most beautiful maidens, Mordecai's hidden Hadassah was discovered. The king's commandment and decree was heard. It could not be resisted. Others had been already gathered, and Esther also was compelled to go.

Alas, what a destiny and prospect seemed to be before her! To a poor, unprotected girl, who loved God and desired to do his will, who had been brought up in his service, and in the purity of his commandments, what prospect could have been more repulsive? To be snatched from the kind protection of the faithful Mordecai, and from a habitation where the word of God, and the voice of prayer and praise had cheered her poverty; where pure and faithful love had made her dinner of herbs better than the feast of the mighty; to be dragged among multitudes as a victim to the arbitrary passions of a heathen king; shut up under his single control, and subject only to his will for life or death; where sin surrounded her on every side, and no servant of God was near,—what prospect could be worse, or more fearful for her? Suppose it to recur to some Christian American or English girl in Burmah or Siam, what youthful Christian female would not say that death was a thousand times to be preferred to such a life as this?

How exposed was she to be to the power of human crime! How wretched in the prospect of her life! We can not wonder that it was only by compulsion she was brought. All the anxieties of her heart and conscience, and all her sense of personal dignity, struggled against a destiny so horrible. What her heavenly Father designed, she knew not. She could only look upon the sorrows of the present, and confide to him the gloom and darkness of the future.

We may well conceive the anguish of her last prayer in the solitary chamber she was never to see again—the grief of her separation from her faithful kinsman—the bitterness of her despair when she took her last look of his humble mansion. How infinitely better is poverty with piety, than luxury with crime. We can hardly conceive of a state more wretched than Esther's, when she was "brought also to the man who had the custody of the king's women," among the multitude of heathen and untaught maidens who were gathered there. All before her was thick darkness, and death would have been welcomed as a blessed deliverance.

But thus God would show how mightily and wisely he performs his work. Thus would he cut off every circumstance of earthly advantage, when he would show us how he could protect and prosper those who put their trust in him. How full of encouragement and strength is such a view of God's wisdom and love. How it should awaken your confidence in his care. How it should establish your choice of his protection and favor. If he is on your side no one can be effectually against you. Learn to choose, to trust, and to obey him alone, and he will carry you safely through every path in which he requires you to go. Keep yourself from voluntary sin, from seeking, or yielding to the power of temptation, and you need have no fear that his protection will fail you, or that he will suffer the evil one to overcome you.

In this exaltation of the captive orphan, God remarkably overruled and employed the wicked passions of men. However he directed the result, and brought great good therefrom according to his will, so far as men were concerned all was sin. The king consulted only his own corrupt desires. His officers combined to minister to his wicked tempers and gratifications. No happiness of others, no peace of violated households, no wretchedness of ruined and discarded

THE MYSTERIOUS BEGINNING. 201

youth, was to be considered as an obstacle in the path. The king's commandment and decree must be obeyed. And Persia must be searched to find the appropriate and satisfying food for his violence and lust.

But God ordered all this wickedness of man to accomplish his own designs of mercy and love. And the history furnishes in this respect a very remarkable illustration of the providence and government of God. Thus he leaves sinful men to follow out their own schemes and wishes, and then he arranges them to produce a result entirely different from any which they had planned for themselves. He has already determined the end to which they shall come, and which he means to attain through their agency, however voluntarily they may act; and then he directs the various streams of their action to flow together till they reach this appointed end.

This does not lessen the wickedness of men. However God may restrain and employ them, their purpose is only to sin. And whatsoever results God may bring out of their wickedness, they must bear the guilt of their sin in the same condemnation. God's mercy may compel them to bless his people, and to glorify himself, while his justice punishes their transgression, and overthrows their own plans of personal gain and glory. What an illustration was there of this in the case of Pharaoh with the Israelites, and in the case of Judas with his divine Master. In each of these, the wickedness of man was great, and God punished their transgression. Yet in each, the results of benefit to others, and of glory to God were also great, and God accomplished his own plans of love and mercy, notwithstanding their interference, and by the very means of their agency. This is his gracious providence working all things according to his own will. "His ways are not as our ways, nor his thoughts as our thoughts."

We can never be permitted to do evil that good may come. The Lord says of such, "their damnation is just." And yet out of the evil which men do, God habitually brings results of benefit, and makes the wrath of man to praise him. Human history abounds with illustrations of this providence of God. How remarkable was the English Reformation from Popery in this respect. Henry the Eighth was a monster of crime. His motives appeared to be his own wicked passions alone. He murdered and he married at his pleasure. Yet God overruled the whole result for the establishment of his truth. This glorious Reformation has been often reproached for Henry's crimes. It would be just as reasonable to reproach the deliverance of the Israelites and their subsequent prosperity, with the crimes of Pharaoh. God set up his Gospel in England by employing the wickedness of Henry to overturn the equal wickedness of the Pope and the priesthood. He made the sins of men to be the instrument of punishing the sins of men. Thus he sets one sinful nation in war to punish another, and thus brings triumphs for humanity and truth out of the very warfare which they wage. Thus he has permitted the crimes of men in the long-continued misery of African slavery. But he has great purposes of good to bring out of this tangled maze of crime. And however his goodness shines in the result for others, the guilt and condemnation of the agents employed remain the same.

Such an illustration of this divine government we have in the history of Esther. God designed to make her an eminent illustration of his goodness to those who trust in him, and an eminent blessing to his people. But to accomplish this purpose, he puts "the wheel in the middle of a wheel." Poor Esther, in her solitary distress, sees the terrible dispensation coming directly over her, apparently for her destruction. God suddenly turns it to move in another direction; and it goes forward to magnify and bless her, and to bless many others through her means. Thus God brings good out of evil, and leads the blind by ways that they know not.

This is a most important lesson. God can make even our own pardoned sins and follies to become a blessing to us, and to bring honor to him. He says to his people, "It shall come to pass that as ye were a curse among the heathen, so will I save you, and ye shall be a blessing." But this abounding mercy can never justify us in a course of sin. It can never make our sin to be any thing but sin. We often feel a strong temptation to think otherwise; to imagine that a good result coming from our transgression may have some influence to make our transgression less guilty. Be careful how you indulge a thought like this. It is a terrible evil to think lightly of your guilt before God. "Fools make a mock at sin." None but fools can do this, so dreadful are the wages and condemnation which it deserves, and the rebellion against a holy God which is involved in it. God calls you to renounce the path of evil, and to walk in the ways of holiness and truth. He commands you to choose him as your portion and your Lord, in the very beginning of your life. Your prosperity on earth will be according to his will. But his blessing will make you rich for ever, and add no sorrow therewith.

Learn then to find your happiness at your Saviour's feet, in the simple and faithful performance of duty for him. Make him the real choice of your heart. The security of his paths is entire. None can harm you, if you are really followers of that which is good. The peace which he gives passes understanding, and the hope which he imparts maketh not ashamed. None are so happy as they who truly dedicate their early youthful hours to Jesus. Make him now your choice. Your past years have been a sufficient record of wasted time, and a heavy responsibility rests upon you for all the privileges which you have already in vain enjoyed. Do not increase this burden by further neglect. Embrace the invitations and promises which the Saviour gives you, as freely as they are offered, and never doubt that on his side you must conquer, and under his protection you must be safe. A far higher promotion than earth can celebrate shall be the portion of those who seek and love him, when earth and time shall be no longer a place or season for them.

XII.

The Important Friendship.

"When a man's ways please the Lord, he maketh even his enemies to be at peace with him."—PROVERBS, xvi. 17.

WHAT principle of divine Providence can be more important than this? To have the friendship of God is to have all that man can ask. If he is on our side, it is of little consequence who may be against us. But he is always on the side of those whose ways please him. If we seek his favor and reconciling love, pardon of sin in that atonement which he hath provided and accepted, the new heart and the right spirit which his Holy Spirit alone can bestow, and if, under his guidance, we strive to walk with him in newness of life, he will make our ways to please him. He will heal our backslidings, bear with our infirmities and crown us with his abounding and everlasting love. Thus shall

all things work together for our good, and even our enemies be found at peace with us.

Esther's history shows us this. In all its aspects her exaltation was most remarkable. But it was attended with illustrations of personal character, of ways which please the Lord, which were equally so, and in every succeeding step her own purity and excellence shone out in a very beautiful and attractive light. The successive facts which made up the process of this exaltation, as exhibiting her own character, we may contemplate with much advantage.

First. Mark the simple cause of this exaltation. It was the divine tribute to her character. Because her ways pleased the Lord, he made her enemies to be at peace with her. He gave her not merely the friendship of hostile persons, but of hostile events also; and the things which should have been for her hurt, were made to promote her prosperity. Who was he that could harm her while she was a follower of that which was good?

We have seen her dragged from her humble home, snatched from Mordecai her only earthly friend, plunged into an abyss that seemed to be inevitable ruin. But she was not only preserved from evil, and guarded from the actual dangers to which she was exposed—all these outward and repulsive facts and agencies were made instruments for her advantage. In every succeeding crisis, she is defended and guarded. She comes out of every trial with increased blessings and gain. In this single aspect her history is very remarkable. And why is this? Her ways pleased the Lord. Her heart had been given in sincere consecration to him. She had chosen his service as her portion and heritage for ever, and he did not forsake her in any hour of her trial.

This is a blessed subject of thought for us. If the Lord be for us, who can be against us? If our gracious Father in heaven justifieth, who is he that condemneth? The friendship of God is all that we can need. And the surest course of prosperity for us is in an affectionate and simple choice of his service and favor as our portion. I earnestly desire to impress this thought upon your minds. You can not adopt it too entirely, nor act upon it too thoroughly. Do you ask for success, for happiness, for final triumph? Do you desire a result of blessedness for this life, and for the life to come! Embrace the hope which the gospel gives. Go to the fountain which the gospel opens. Enter into the Saviour's ranks and belong to him. He will carry you safely through every trial and every contest. He will make all grace abound upon you so that you shall come behind in no gift or blessing that you need. You need have no other care than this. Fix all your watchfulness and all your desire on the one point of being a true follower of the Lord Jesus, having your heart and your hopes with him, and he will guide you safely by his counsel and afterward receive you joyfully to glory.

Second. Mark the way in which this exaltation was accomplished. God gave her favor in the sight of others. In every succeeding step her enemies were found at peace with her. An unseen influence and power preceded her in the path through which she was led and prepared her way before her, so that the evils which she anticipated were all averted, and light beamed forth from the darkness surrounding her at every step she took.

We have followed her to her new abode, and we imagine the distress of her orphan heart as she was carried to the king's house. All that was hopeful, peaceful and happy in life seemed to have departed for ever. Like a poor struggling bird held in the hand by force, she panted for deliverance. How her inmost soul cried out in the words of her native Psalmist, "O, that I had wings like a dove! Then would I fly away and be at rest. I would hasten my escape from the windy storm and tempest." But there could be no resistance. She might "weep sore in the night, and her tears be on her cheeks," but "she had none to comfort her." Though a "precious daughter of Zion, comparable to fine gold, she is esteemed as an earthen pitcher, the work of the hands of the potter." Her sadness and fear would know no bounds, and none but the God of her fathers, in whom she trusted, could be her protection and defense.

But God did not and would not forsake her.

And now we see the beginning of the turning tide. "When a man's ways please the Lord, he maketh even his enemies to be at peace with him." "The maiden pleased Hegai, the keeper of the women, and she obtained kindness of him." Every thing now is to be in her favor. No time is to be lost in her way to the throne which God designed to give her; and all succeeding events shall flow together in a current of advancing prosperity for her. "The best place in the house of the women" is assigned to her "Seven maidens meet to be given to her out of the king's house" are appointed her attendants. All things supposed to be appropriate to her new condition are at once bestowed upon her. Kindness and respect surrounded her, and her fears were in a degree alleviated. So that to a mere sensual and earthly mind her condition would appear luxurious and desirable.

Yet with all this accumulation of attentions and kindness, to her youthful heart and pure mind her apparent exaltation was only repulsive and dreadful. Far rather would she have been with Mordecai in the loneliness of his godly habitation, than amidst all the luxury and glare of this royal palace. But the future was to her all unknown, and no gleam of light yet appeared to explain the mystery of her condition. Yet God was her protector and her friend, and in the protection of the Lord of Hosts she found her only and all-sufficient comfort. Amidst all the splendors of her outward condition, her sinking heart could only trust itself to him.

So easily can your gracious, heavenly Father change and order the minds of others concerning you. He can make all your enemies at peace with you. With all this government of his you have nothing to do. Dwell in the land of his appointment according to his will contentedly and thankfully, and be doing good as he shall open the way and his Word shall direct. The care and government of all is in his hands. The responsibility of the control is on his shoulders. You have only to go forward in the path of duty, and to trust in him without fear or doubt. He will make all things work together for good to them that love him. His habitual method of blessing his children is by moving the hearts of others to favor them, and by raising up friends to defend and provide for them in their necessities. Thus he prepared Pharaoh's daughter to be the defender and the royal nurse for the infant Moses. Thus he raised up friends for David in his successive persecutions, and made the things which were devised for his hurt to turn out for his advantage. Thus also he dealt with Daniel and his companions. And thus will he deal with you.

He gives a pleasant and attractive aspect to religious character, adorns it by his Spirit with traits of meekness and spiritual beauty, makes its influence agreeable and pleasant to those who become connected with it, and in this way makes his servants acceptable to others, and a real blessing to many. This system of his gracious government lays out the line of personal duty for you. It is your duty to be a blessing to all persons and at all times. Make your religion attractive, your manners gentle and affectionate, your heart sympathizing, forgiving, benevolent. If you are persecuted or opposed, be sure that you are persecuted for righteousness' sake. Thus will you honor your God and Saviour and be yourself blessed and prosperous. Thus will your enemies be made at peace with you, and others will be made to bless you by his own power and grace.

Third. Mark the state of mind which true piety will display under the most trying circumstances. This was beautifully exhibited in Esther as she passed through the trying ordeal which was to lead to her exaltation. They who live in the Spirit will walk in the Spirit, and will bring forth the fruits of the Spirit appropriate to it in every new condition and trial of life.

Esther showed great self-respect. The dignity of her own personal character she would not sacrifice. She would not " show her people, or her kindred, for Mordecai had charged her that she should not show it." Mordecai's experience of life had taught him the bitterness of the prejudice and hostility of the wicked against the people of God. There would have been no hope of the exaltation of Esther in that heathen place, or of her deliverance from it, in Mordecai's view, had she announced that she was a poor Jewish captive.

She could hope for nothing but to be immediately cast out in a permanently degraded and neglected position. She therefore silently and quietly endured the will of God in the trying condition in which she was placed, and maintained, in all the seclusion she could obtain, her own dignity of personal character.

What is so dignified and refining as true piety? It habitually clothes the character with grace and purity, and the manners with delicacy and elegance. The dwelling of the Spirit in the heart produces ever "whatsoever things are true, whatsoever things are honorable, just, pure, lovely, and of good report," and "if there be any virtue or any praise," his work leads to the acquisition and maintenance of these things. We see the poorest daughters of earth exalted by the transforming power of true religion, to a hold on the reverence of all, and often to the admiration and delight of many. True piety is patient, quiet and unassuming. But it will not, and it need not yield to the scornful and unjust prejudice of the world by publishing its own lowly origin in earthly things, or the poverty of its connections in earthly relations, if these facts have been the will of God concerning it.

Esther showed a quiet submission to the will of God. She asked for nothing. She desired nothing of all that she saw around her. All the state and magnificence of her new condition were nothing to her. Her mind could find repose only in God. Her unseen but gracious friend was the only friend remaining to her now. "Mordecai walked every day before the court of the women's house to know how Esther did and what should become of her." But she could see Mordecai no more. Her only earthly friend the arbitrary rules of her splendid prison house had shut entirely out from her. She had no sympathy from those around her. They had not her principles. They could not understand her heart. They could only envy and admire what their low conceptions considered her happy lot. The things which she abhorred they had been taught and accustomed to regard as desirable and delightful. Thus completely alone, to whom could she look but unto God? Her case was one of great trial, trial for which there appeared no earthly alleviation. But it was trial which none but a pure and religious mind could comprehend, and it was vain to speak of it to any who listened to her there. To whom could she go but to him who had the words of eternal life? Her heart rested on God alone, and there she was at peace. Her father's God could and would protect and deliver her in his own time and way; and with that assurance she was contented and submissive.

How beautiful is such an example. Remember that divine promise, Isaiah, xxvi. 3: "Thou wilt keep him in perfect peace, whose mind is stayed on thee, because he trusteth in thee. Trust ye in the Lord for ever, for in the Lord Jehovah is everlasting strength." Thus true religion reposes in the day of trial. It leans its hope upon God, and is at rest. "In every thing by prayer and supplication with thanksgiving it makes known its requests unto God; and the peace of God, which passeth all understanding, keeps the heart and mind through Christ Jesus." (Philippians, iv. 6.) We see

THE IMPORTANT FRIENDSHIP. 219

this spirit exemplified in Esther's course, and we behold the blessedness of the result.

Esther showed entire indifference to worldly display. There was a preparation appointed for these victims of the royal pleasure, through which, according to the rules of Eastern luxury, each must pass. But there was also an additional provision for individual choice to enlarge the means of personal decoration, as each might desire. "Thus came every maiden unto the king. Whatsoever she desired was given to her, to go with her out of the house of the women unto the king's house." But "when the turn of Esther was come to go in unto the king, she required nothing but what Hegai, the king's chamberlain, appointed." She desired no adorning. She asked for no peculiar ornaments. That which was appointed for her by the authority which held her in captivity she was required to receive, and she would receive it with patience. This was a part of the divine arrangement in her trial, and she bowed to it as the will of God who had placed her there and would protect her there, in the quietness of an uncomplaining spirit. But she had laid out no plans for herself. She had no conquest to make, no ends to accomplish for herself. She would make no effort to enhance the beauty with which God had been pleased to endow her. She was contented to leave her whole influence and prospects in her Father's hands, and therefore, "she required nothing." This was true modesty, as well as a simple and pious trust in God. Her mind and thoughts were directed to him, not to herself. And whether she should be made to appear attractive in the eyes of men or not, his holy will concerning her would be done.

What an example was this to youth in the midst of the snares and artificial glare of the world! True adorning is "not the outward adorning of plaiting the hair, and of wearing of gold, or of putting on apparel, but it is in the hidden man of the heart, in that which is not corruptible, even the ornament of a meek and quiet spirit, which is in the sight of God of great price." What attractive beauty there is in a heavenly temper, a lowly spiritual mind!

This is a jewel of the Lord's preparation and appointment, and eminently becomes and adorns the children of God. And thus true piety in youth will manifest itself in its intercourse with the world. Its delicacy and Christian modesty asks for no display, and imagines no observation. But vanity, prompting a diffidence which is the very opposite of modesty, seeks for much outward enhancement and help. That extravagance and indelicacy of female dress which abounds in worldly society can not comport with the simplicity of life and character which belong to the children of God. A heart truly set on God, and trusting in him requires nothing for itself, thinks not of dressing or appearing for other eyes, and neither courts nor desires the admiration or the gaze of the sensual or the silly.

Esther showed a simple and entire trust in God. In the bitterness of her heart's sorrow she had no other protector. But He was her sun and her shield, and her heart trusted in him. Her thoughts and her prayers were with the faithful Mordecai, whose solicitude and distress could be relieved and comforted only by the peace of his simple walk with God. With him she lifted up her eyes unto the Lord their God, who only could preserve them from all evil and be their portion for ever. Every thing around the captive orphan was dark and discouraging. Things seen could give her no relief. Her hope must fasten itself on an unseen God alone. There only could she be at rest.

In such a condition there is no other refuge for us. We must roll ourselves upon God, cast our burden upon him, and leave our welfare entirely in his hands. But this is enough. A simple, filial faith triumphs over every obstacle and every fear. He will never fail nor forsake those who put their trust in him. There Esther rested in the day of her calamity, and was kept in peace. God, even her own God, was reigning over all things around her, and in the fullness of his protecting love she could abide and calmly trust. It was a beautiful exhibition of character, and we do not wonder when we read, in such a history, that "Esther obtained favor in the sight of all them that looked upon her." Such a faithful trusting servant of God is perfectly secure in the midst of a world of sin. While such a course of conduct always adorns the doctrine of God the Saviour, it will also command the homage and confidence of men.

What have you then to do, my dear young friends, but thus simply to walk with God? Maintain his cause faithfully and affectionately, and he will make your enemies to be at peace with you. You shall be safe under his protection, and happy in his love. His goodness and mercy will crown your daily path, and make all things work together for good to you. "Your peace shall flow down like a river, your righteousness shall be as the waves of the sea," and his everlasting love will acknowledge you as his own in that day when he maketh up his jewels in his eternal glory.

XIII.

The Guardianship of Grace.

"He preserveth the souls of his saints; he delivereth them out of the hand of the wicked."—Psalm xcvii. 10.

Providence and Grace have two separate dominions. The providence of God rules over outward things for the welfare of his children. The grace of God redeems, renews, governs and preserves their own inward heart and character. Both are the subjects of covenant and earnest promises to them. All things shall work together for their good. He will never fail them nor forsake them. They shall never perish, and no one shall pluck them out of his hand. He "will guide them by his counsel, and afterward receive them to glory."

These two merciful arrangements are never separated from each other in the experience of the children of God. Their heavenly Father protects them in their outward walk in life from

THE GUARDIANSHIP OF GRACE. 225

danger; and sanctifies and delivers them in their own inward experience from the power and temptations of sin in the peculiar trials which they meet.

One part of this gracious work we have seen in Esther's case. God protected and preserved the captive orphan by his own power. She had been taught to love him, to hate evil. Her heart was really given to God. But she was now cast into the midst of great perils, and exposed to great temptations. Yet the Lord whom she loved will not forsake her. He has thus far delivered her from the hands of the wicked, and he will protect and guide her even to the end. Mordecai's fears and anxieties concerning her have been relieved and answered by the Lord of all. And all the elements of her own character are the evidences of the grace and power of her Lord.

There is something extremely beautiful and even grand in this exhibition of youthful piety. Its perfect modesty, its quiet trust, its conscious elevation, its peaceful walk in the midst of danger, combine to present a lovely and attractive example. Few will be carried through the extremes of Esther's trial. But the world is full of illustrations of the same powers and instruments of temptation, and too frequently exhibits a sad and ruinous yielding to their control. Yet all do not yield. The church of God has furnished many illustrations of a calm and victorious enduring of such assaults; and of the blessed results of character strengthened and established by the contests which they bring. God preserves the souls of his saints. He keeps his little ones in the hollow of his hand and delivers them from the power of the evil one.

In our contemplation of the instance of such protection before us, we have followed our friendless orphan to the royal house of Ahasuerus. We have now to mark her course and character there. Thus far we have seen Esther the lovely captive girl, and Esther the youthful servant of God defended in the midst of temptation and danger. Now we are to look upon Esther, the Queen of Persia, and see how God fulfills all his promises, and protects and maintains in usefulness and happiness the souls of his servants.

In this view, we see first, true piety in worldly exaltation. This exaltation has been brought about by a remarkable train of circumstances in the good providence of God. Every probability was against it, and nothing could be more unlikely than the result which was thus produced. But God fulfills his own purposes in his own way. He places the wheel in the middle of the wheel, by his gracious government, working in the midst of human schemes, overruling and directing them all to accomplish his own designs. "The king loved Esther above all the women, and she obtained grace and favor in his sight more than all the virgins; so that he set the crown royal on her head, and made her queen instead of Vashti."

Remarkable as this result was in itself, the reason given for it is yet more worthy of our attention. "She obtained grace and favor in his sight." Her exaltation is ascribed to a far higher power than any that outwardly appeared. God was ruling and ordering it in his own way, and according to his own will. Esther's exaltation is not attributed merely to her own beauty, however great her personal attractions might have been, still less to any arts or additions of taste and skill to increase the power of these attractions, all which she had refused entirely; but directly to the grace and favor of God. It is he that maketh peace in the borders of his people, and giveth them favor in the sight of those who rule them; and how blessed and valuable is such a relation to him, and such an assurance of his love and favor.

You may carry out this principle in all your expectations and plans of life. Your youthful hearts desire earthly success. Prosperity and elevation in your various walks in life seem to you always an object worthy of your pursuit and toil. God may surely give it to you. But he would have you realize that it is his gift. The wise and the only sure way to make the earth a blessing to you, is to seek his favor with it. Choose his side as yours at the very outset of life. This will bring you the measure of earthly gain and glory which he seeth best for you.

But it will also, which is far more, make the earthly substance which you do gain a real and permanent blessing to you.

But surely there is a higher exaltation than any which is wholly confined to earth. There is a throne above all earthly thrones for those who conquer in the Saviour's host. This God reserveth for those who love him. They who find grace and favor in his sight are made partakers of the heavenly exaltation. Seek this throne and kingdom, the kingdom of God and his righteousness. This is the more excellent way. Make your possession of it sure. You may partake of no earthly exaltation; your path here may be lowly and suffering in the shades of darkness and sorrow. This will be the appointment of your heavenly Father for you. Be contented with it. Lose what you may, be sure that you do not lose the glory which God giveth to his saints, nor fail to gain your portion in that kingdom which can not be moved.

The king of Persia made a royal feast at Esther's exaltation. It was a feast of far different character from that which preceded the downfall of Vashti. "The king made a great feast unto all his princes and his servants, even Esther's feast; and he made a release to the provinces, and gave gifts according to the state of the king." The former feast was distinguished by abounding selfish, sensual indulgence. This was marked by releases, gifts and acts of favor to the destitute and the suffering, distributed in the richest and freest abundance. Ahasuerus' feast was the gratification of vanity and lust; Esther's feast was the token of the exaltation of the righteous, when all the people rejoice. The people of God are always made a blessing to men, in the influence which they exercise; and in their final exaltation among men, when the kingdoms of the earth shall be given to the saints of the Most High, the most abounding gifts and mercies shall be showered upon the world around. My dear young friends, seek your exaltation with them. If God shall give you the high places of the earth, so improve and employ your influence here, that others may have reason to bless God in your behalf. And even if in the things of earth you are still among the lowly, according to his will, you may yet be a blessing in your example and influence to multitudes, and though poor, may make many rich.

Second. We see here the emptiness of earthly contrasts. The difference between the two conditions in which Esther is presented, is wonderful indeed. No earthly contrast could be greater than between a poor Jewish captive orphan, amidst the oppressions of a heathen land, and the queen of all the provinces of the kingdom of Persia. Yet all this is nothing when viewed in relation to the power and greatness of God. This transformation, and far more than this, he is able to accomplish with a word, for those whom he loves. The difference in the importance or the honor of the two stations is nothing to him. He is no respecter of persons, and Esther as a queen is no more to him than Esther as a captive. Man looks upon the outward appearance. God looketh upon the heart. Let us seek to gain his mind, and learn to value others, and to think of ourselves, according to the reality of character, and not according to the mere appendages and aspects of the outward condition.

The vain mind of youth delights in worldly elevation and grandeur. And even under the teaching of the Holy Spirit, this tendency to desire and delight in outward appearances, long resists control and strives for the preëminence. But Esther's trials of character will be far greater in her new condition than in her former one. Few can bear great earthly prosperity with advantage. Many whose characters have shined brightly in the beauty and fruitfulness of true religion, in the season of affliction, and in the low estate of life, have grown dim and discouraging amidst the temptations of prosperity. It is here that the principle of our text comes in, "he preserveth the souls of his saints." The gracious God keeps those who love him, in the hour of temptation, from the power of evil. He delivers them from the destructive influence which surrounds them. He carries them safely through the hour of trial and makes their graces to shine the brighter in every new condition in which he is pleased to try them. The Spirit of God supports his children amidst the temptations of earthly exaltation and enables them to adorn the doctrine of the Saviour whom they profess to serve. Yet no one who has tried or seen the influence of a prosperous condition on the mind and character of man can doubt that the strongest temptations and the heaviest contests for the soul are there. God displays the riches and wonders of his grace in thus defending and guarding his chosen ones in the dangers of this contest.

Prosperity brings in the claims of worldly fashion, the examples of the exalted wicked, the hostility of a world which at the same time tempts to transgression, and scoffs at fidelity. It introduces a multitude of new thoughts and new relations which corrupt the character and entangle the soul. It makes new provisions and offers new inducements for the indulgence of those fleshly lusts which war against the soul and so often drown men in perdition. The life of piety declines. The spirit of prayer grows dull. The habit of prayer fails. The modesty of dress and personal appearance is laid aside. The purity of the outward walk is disregarded. The young professor becomes a backslider, a wanderer from God, and at last an apostate. The earnest spiritual walk has gone, driven away by the corrupting influence of the world in its means and provisions for sensual enjoyment. The whole character and current of life become sometimes transformed from apparent light to extreme darkness. And thus in many an hour of sorrow the fallen youth looks back to long for the earlier condition of poverty, quietness and protection. When the wants were few the hopes were bright, and the peace of God ruled in the conscience and the heart.

So often do we see this course of declension and this result of sorrow, as earthly prosperity with its temptations and offerings comes upon the youthful professor of religion, that we regard the change as full of trials and perhaps the most dangerous to which we are subjected. A friend of the eminent Mr. Cecil called upon him one day to ask for his congratulations on a large and unexpected increase of wealth which he had received. Mr. Cecil replied, "I will pray for you as a friend under temptation." How well do we pray in our Litany for God's deliverance of us, " in all time of our prosperity," as well as " in all time of our tribulation." And when young Christians long for a larger measure of earthly wealth and earthly pleasures, let them remember that the change they seek is more full of dangers than of joys, and in the spirit of contentment seek that divine blessing which maketh truly rich, and addeth no sorrow therewith.

Third. We see in Esther's case that under the divine guidance and grace true piety may pass uninjured through every state. When God himself arranges and imposes the trial, he will always provide a way of escape for those who truly love him, that they may be able to bear it. Esther's sudden exaltation had no effect on her fidelity to God, or on her attachment to his people. We see the same guarded self-respect, and the same love for Mordecai afterwards as before. " When the virgins were gathered together the second time, then Mordecai sat in the king's gate. Esther had not yet showed her kindred or her people, as Mordecai had charged her; for Esther did the commandment of Mordecai as when she was brought up with him." Though she could see him no more, she did not forget the precious principles of piety and truth which she had learned from him. Her renewed heart, and her humble and consistent walk of faith remained the same amidst all the temptations of her new condition. Such a holy and beautiful character adorns a throne far more than a throne can exalt it. It has a beauty and power exclusively its own. Whether high or low in the stations of this world, this work of the Holy Spirit in the heart has a real dignity belonging to it, that can nowhere else be found. It wears the image of divine holiness. It displays the workmanship of divine power. It adorns and honors the grace which it enjoys, and the character which it has received.

The proportioned usefulness of individual piety in different stations in human life, it would be very difficult to decide. God often selects the feeblest instruments as the most important agencies to promote his glory. We may therefore dismiss all anxiety about the influence of our appointed station. We have only to fill up the measure of our own position in the duties which God has been pleased to assign us, and leave the result entirely to him. He will give the blessing according to his own will. But what can show more beautifully the reality of the work of God in the heart, than the constant exercise and display of the same kindness, tenderness and simplicity in a high estate, as in a previous low condition. One of the most striking facts in Esther's character is this repeated assertion of her faithful remembrance of Mordecai, and of her permanent regard to his instructions. This work of the Holy Spirit upon her heart followed her and protected her in all the experience of her exaltation. Even in the glory of her kingdom she could not forget the faithful guardian and instructor of her youth. Ah, what a blessing do we confer, when we succeed, under the sovereign power of the Holy Spirit, in laying up in the youthful mind the principles of true religion and real love for God! This is something real, a gift that will abide. Years may pass, changes may come; we may not live on earth to see the result of our labors. But we have been God's intruments in imparting undying principles of truth, the power of an eternal life, and God will surely own and bless them, and bring out from them the blessing in which multitudes shall rejoice. The harvest of the seed which we sow may be far distant, but it will surely come. It may be that, like Mordecai, we have educated and prepared a mind for a coming state of influence and earthly power far beyond any conceptions of ours. It is certain we have made ready the way, in the degree of our faithful and appropriate labors, for an exaltation and happiness eternal in the heavens. The work of grace which God begins, he carries on even to the end, and in due season we shall reap a harvest for our own abundant satisfaction, if we faint not.

Fourth, we see Esther's exaltation marked by sincere gratitude and affectionate care for the appointed instrument of it. Her first recorded relation to the king who had raised her up to the throne, was as the preserver of his life. The history of this immediately succeeds. " In those days, while Mordecai sat in the king's gate, two of the king's chamberlains of those which kept the door, were wroth, and sought to lay hands on the king Ahasuerus, and the thing was known to Mordecai, who told it unto Esther the queen, and Esther certified the king thereof in Mordecai's name. And when inquisition was made of the matter, it was found out; therefore they were both hanged on a tree. And it was written in the book of the Chronicles before the king."

This was a beautiful illustration of the gratitude which attends real and lofty piety. A low and upstart mind hates to acknowledge obligations; nay, often feels a new hostility towards those from whom benefits have been received. But a truly great and exalted mind forgets no benefits that have been conferred, and esteems it a high privilege to be able to pay them directly back to the person who has bestowed them. Esther acknowledges her twofold obligation, while she gives the information which saves the life of the king, and gives it in the name of Mordecai, that it might in some way be made the instrument of promoting his advantage, and of rescuing him from the poverty of his condition.

This gratitude for kindness from our fellow men is always characteristic of true piety. A religious heart is ashamed of no obligations, thankful for all the acts and expressions of tenderness, humble under all gifts, rejoicing in the ability to be useful, delighting to communicate to others the happiness itself enjoys. Even if the immediate agents and givers of its bounties are beyond its reach, the obligations are by no means forgotten. They will be repaid at any distance of time, to any proper representatives of the original benefactor. And if such can not be found the same spirit will lead to a constant imparting to the needy and the destitute within its reach, the utmost measure of usefulness and kindness, as a just acknowledgment of the blessings which it has itself received from the gracious hand of God.

Let me press the consideration of this lovely pattern and character upon your minds, and urge your earnest and cordial imitation of it. Shun that sinful pride which hates the feeling and the acknowledgment of dependence. Every expression of kindness on the part of our fellow-men, all those acts and words of tenderness, which are so multiplied in our experience, and which make our lives so often a constant current of happiness and enjoyment, combine to lay upon us a heavy obligation of gratitude and usefulness to others. And it ought to be a source of delight to us, just as constant and just as fresh in our habitual experience, to acknowledge our obligations, to be thankful for the love of all, and to carry out in our relations to others the same spirit of cordial benevolence and of liberal aid and encouragement. A joyful, and pleasant thing it is to be thankful. And a beautiful and effective element of real piety is always in the spirit which delights in gratitude, and which loves to speak and to act towards all in cheerful payment of the debts we thus owe.

But if gratitude to earthly friends and benefactors so truly becomes us, how much more the spirit of thankfulness to that heavenly Friend whose gifts all earthly agencies for our comfort are. He is the brother born for our adversity, who by his own death has given to us eternal life; and becoming a servant in our likeness, has exalted us to reign as kings with him. How unspeakable are our obligations to him! In his blood we have divine forgiveness; in his gracious protection, divine defense; in his glorious reign, eternal life and glory. Let his love to you constrain a return of earnest love for him. Strive to feel and delight to own your obligations to him every day. Be not content to be at a distance from him. While multitudes still conspire against him, and crucify him daily afresh, let the record of your fidelity to him be in the chronicles of his kingdom, and stand as the evidence of your sincere faith in his promises, and your devoted love for his service. Soon that great record will be brought out in a public proclamation, and happy will be the annunciation for you, as an acceptance of your character and service, "Inasmuch as ye did it unto one of the least of these, my brethren, ye did it unto me; enter ye into the joy of your Lord." Nothing that you have done for him shall be forgotten. He will never be unrighteous, in refusing to acknowledge the labors of love which you have showed for his name's sake, in your affectionate and faithful efforts to do his will.

XIV.

The Time for Usefulness.

"Who knoweth whether thou art come to the kingdom for such a time as this?"—Esther, iv. 14.

This text discloses another very important principle in the divine providence, which we learn in this chamber of true religion. Our times are in the Lord's hands. He fixes the bounds of our habitations, and arranges our conditions according to his own will. His servants have a special earthly calling wherein they are called, the duties of which they are individually to fulfill, and a particular temporal dispensation committed to them, the obligations of which they must personally bear. God thus graciously arranges, according to his own design, both the nature and the circumstances of their personal duties. He has particular relative objects to secure in the exaltation of those whom he loves. No one lives for himself alone. And when any of his servants are raised to influence, or wealth, or power, it is that he may make them effective instruments of his power for blessing to others. They have the privilege of being workers together with him, in helping their fellow-men, and of participating in the gratitude which he receives from the poor whom he hath relieved, or the oppressed whom he hath set free.

There is, therefore, a special propriety of time, at which his gifts of power and influence are bestowed upon particular men. If one is made rich, it is because there are many poor waiting to be enriched by him, and he is to have the greater blessing of imparting, giving to his fellow-men. There is a particular reason, could we know it, for which we are "come to the kingdom for such a time." We should study our duty in the circumstances of its time, the particular calls and opportunities for our labor in the Lord's cause, the openings which are especially furnished in that time for appointed usefulness to our fellow-men. The circumstances of the time and the characters of the agents have a mutual action upon each other, so that the times seem to make the men they call for, and the men mark the character of the age in which they live.

This principle of divine appointment we see in the captive orphan. We have seen her exalted to the height of earthly dignity and power, carrying with her the same unchanging spirit of piety and true devotion to God into the new trials of her unexpected exaltation. Every virtue and trait of holiness in her character shines with increasing brightness and beauty as she goes forward in her appointed dispensation. And we come now to consider the purposes of her exaltation. Why was this captive orphan made the Queen of Persia?

Mordecai evidently discerns a purpose for this remarkable providence in the circumstances of the time in which they were living. "Who knoweth whether thou art come to the kingdom for such a time as this?" There had come a period in the history of her own people, when just the influence which she could exercise was required, and she had been manifestly raised to the kingdom to meet the demands and obligations of such a time. The fidelity and success with which she was able to do this, her subsequent history relates. Let us consider the circumstances of the time.

First, it was a time of great trial for the people of Israel. Haman, of whom we are to speak hereafter, had planned a scheme for their complete destruction. "All the king's servants that were in the king's gate bowed and reverenced Haman, for the king had so commanded. But Mordecai bowed not, nor did him reverence." In his hatred for Mordecai for this affront, Haman resolved to destroy all the people of Mordecai's nation as well as him. "When Haman saw that Mordecai bowed not, nor did him reverence, then was Haman full of wrath; and he thought scorn to lay hands on Mordecai alone, for they had showed him the people of Mordecai; wherefore Haman sought to destroy all the Jews that were throughout the whole kingdom of Ahasuerus, even the people of Mordecai." This captive people were placed entirely in his hands. By false accusation against them he obtained the king's permission for their destruction. "Haman said unto King Ahasuerus, There is a certain people scattered abroad and dispersed among the people in all the provinces of the kingdom, and their laws are diverse from all people; neither keep they the king's laws, therefore it is not for the king's credit to suffer them. If it please the king let it be written that they may be destroyed, and I will pay ten thousand talents of silver in the hands of those that have the charge of the business, to bring into the king's treasuries. And the king took the ring from his hand and gave it unto Haman, the Jews' enemy. And the king said unto Haman, The silver is given to thee, the people also, to do with them as it seemeth good to thee. And the letters were sent by posts into all the king's provinces to destroy, to kill, and cause to perish all Jews, both young and old, little children and women in one day, and to take the spoil of them for a prey." Thus the decree had gone forth for their ruin and there seemed no method of possible deliverance. Mordecai "beheld the tears of such as were oppressed, and they had no comforter; and on the side of their oppressors there was power, but they had no comforter." At such a time was his orphan ward exalted to the throne of Persia.

Thus the Lord often shuts up his people to the exercise of a simple faith in his own power and defense. There seems no method of escape. The wheel of his providence appears rolling forward for their destruction. It is like Ezekiel's wheel, high and terrible, beyond any power or skill of man in resistance. Their hearts are brought into despair, and having no other hope their souls look up to him who never refuses to hear the cry of his servants. Suddenly "the wheel in the middle of the wheel" is seen in motion. A way of deliverance wholly unexpected is laid open, and God interposes as the special and mighty protector of those who trust in him. Thus was it with the Israelites at the Red Sea. They saw the Egyptians marching after them, and the sea before them, and " they were sore afraid, and the children of Israel cried unto the Lord." But "Moses said unto the people, Fear ye not, stand still, and see the salvation of God, which he will show to you to-day; for the Egyptians whom ye have seen to-day ye shall see them again no more for ever." They saw no way of escape from certain death. But God became their redeemer and their defense in a new and unexpected way of triumph.

There was great distress among the Jews in Persia. "In every province, whithersoever the king's commandment and his decree came, there was great mourning among the Jews, and fasting, and weeping and wailing, and many lay in sackcloth and ashes." Their sorrows and fears drove them in humble, united prayer to God, and in this earnest humiliation before him, he heard their cry. "When Mordecai perceived all that was done, Mordecai rent his clothes, and put on sackcloth and ashes, and went out in the midst of the city, and cried with a loud and bitter cry, and came even before the king's gate, for none might enter into the king's gate clothed with sackcloth."

A time of greater trial to a people, or circumstances of more overwhelming distress than these could hardly be imagined. At such a time, Esther had come to the kingdom. The earnest, sorrowful cry of her faithful kinsman, she could not hear, for her luxury was to be interrupted by no such sounds of woe. But the strange facts were made the subject of conversation within her palace, and " Esther's maids and chamberlains came and told her." They little knew the interest she felt in the stories they brought, for they were ignorant of her relation to Mordecai. But her own heart felt the instant burden, and longed for some method of relief.

Thus God prepared the dispensation she was to fulfill, and made her ready for the great work she was to accomplish in it. As yet she little thought of all she had to do in her new position, and we may trace the steps by which she was prepared for the work which was already prepared for her.

Second, the time tested the sincerity of Esther's affection for Mordecai, and brought that into immediate demonstration. His distress pierced her heart, and whatever might be the cause of his sorrows, then unknown to her, it was impossible that they should be unnoticed by her. So we read in the history, " Then was the queen exceedingly grieved and she sent raiment to clothe Mordecai, and to take away his sackcloth from him; but he received it not." This refusal of her kindness made the case more painful still. "Then called Esther for Hatach, one of the king's chamberlains, whom he had appointed to attend upon her, and gave him a commandment to Mordecai, to know what it was, and why it was."

How beautiful was this grateful kindness to her faithful friend! Does human tenderness ever appear more attractive and honorable than in circumstances like these? The highest exaltation in earthly things acknowledging its obligations for the benefit of the past. But this is the habitual fruit of true religion, and it is in such manifestations of their character and real excellence that "wisdom is justified of all her children." Certainly there is much in the pride of the heart which resists a renewed spirit like this. But it can never be witnessed without being commended and honored by men, however unable to imitate it.

The eminent Archbishop Tillotson was the

son of a plain Yorkshire farmer. After he had been elevated to his high position in the church, his father came to Lambeth to visit him in his new residence. The servants hesitated at his uncourtly aspect and dress, and refused to admit him. The archbishop coming to the entrance of the palace at the time, earnestly rebuked the assumption of his servants, and knelt down before the venerable man, and implored his blessing, and then announced to his astonished attendants that the poor man to whom they had refused admittance to the house was his own father.

Another excellent man in England, Bishop Humphrey, was riding through Lincolnshire, in his carriage, when suddenly he ordered his servants to stop, and descending from the carriage, he crossed silently into a field, and knelt down upon the ground. After he had continued sometime in prayer, he returned to his carriage, and said to his attendants, "Many years ago, when I was a poor boy, I was watching cattle in this field, and on one frosty morning I drove up a cow who had been lying on that spot all night that I might warm my bare feet on the ground beneath her, and I could not pass the place without going to thank God there for all the mercies I have since received from his hands."

These are blessed and lovely fruits of the Holy Spirit, and are worthy of your earnest thought and imitation. Thus Esther displays the gratitude of her affectionate heart. Her exalted position has produced no forgetfulness of her former poverty, and cultivated no assumption of greatness or distinction in consequence of her attainment of power. Mordecai is just as dear to her, and as honored by her, as before. And her time of usefulness is marked by the exercise and display of this special work of grace upon her heart. Those who honor God, he will honor. And wherever there are such manifest proofs of grace, such evidences not only of a new heart, but of peculiar adaptation to honor the profession which is made, God has prepared the possessors for special usefulness, and prepared some special openings for usefulness to others for them. They have come to the throne for such a time as this.

Third. The time also tried the sincerity of Esther's affection for her nation. Mordecai returns, by her messenger, a full account of the difficulty and sorrow which had arisen for her people. He gave him also "a copy of the writing, of the decree, that had been given at Shushan to destroy the Jews, to show it unto Esther, and to declare it unto her, and to charge her that she should go in unto the king, to make supplication unto him, and to make request before him for her people." This information and request greatly increased the grief and the difficulties of Esther. She had not yet made her origin or her connections known. To take the open part of this condemned nation now, when they were outcast and without an advocate, might be most inconvenient and dangerous to her. Her distress was great; but her secluded position rendered any interference on her part a question of great difficulty and doubt.

Again she sends her messenger to Mordecai —"All the king's servants, and the people of the king's provinces do know, that whosoever, whether man or woman, shall come unto the king, into the inner court, who is not called, there is one law of his to put him to death, except such to whom the king shall hold out the golden scepter, that he may live; but I have not been called to come in unto the king these thirty days." Mordecai replies to her objection of the danger of her compliance with his request, "Think not with thyself that thou shalt escape in the king's house, more than all the Jews." Her personal danger might be as great there as elsewhere. But a still more important reason for her utmost effort, was her duty to that divine providence which had raised her to the throne, apparently for some crisis like the very one which had now arisen. Mordecai is not in despair in reference to his nation. He has still entire confidence in the divine protection and blessing. God will not forsake the people of his choice. Accordingly, Mordecai says to Esther, "If thou altogether holdest thy peace at this time, then shall there enlargement and deliverance arise to the Jews from another place; but thou and thy father's house shall be destroyed; and who knoweth whether thou art come to the kingdom for such a time as this?" This call upon her conscience and her sense of duty Esther could not refuse. She felt the force of the truth presented. God had exalted her to be a blessing to his people, to whom she felt the tenderest attachment, and without further hesitation she resolves to enter upon the plan of defense and rescue for them, dangerous as it might be.

This was the action of love for her own nation, in their special relation to herself. The truly pious heart will cherish an universal love. The wants and sorrows of all mankind are the subjects of its sympathy and its concern. This is the controlling spirit of the gospel; a love for all mankind, and a desire to be useful to all, as God shall open the means and ways. Wherever there is suffering to be relieved, whether bodily or mental, there the Christian heart acknowledges a claim and an obligation; and if the relief be within the limit of its powers, and the reach of its influence, there will be a cheerfulness and delight in its ministration.

But true religion especially exalts and enlarges domestic love, and love for our country and nation. The more truly the heart is engaged for God the more earnestly will it feel the sorrows and needs of those who are near to us. Have we wealth? We have those connected with us who are poor and suffering. Have we station or knowledge? We can not overpass the ignorance of our own connections or country to expend all our means or efforts on those who are far distant. There may be two extremes in such relations of duty; the entire exclusion of the wider work on the one side and the neglect of the domestic duty on the other. Indifference on the part of Christians to the whole of relative obligations we can not imagine. It is no Christian heart which has no fellowship in suffering and no tenderness for woe. Yet we sadly see a hardness of heart often attendant on exalted conditions. Men seem to feel that they have been elevated by their own efforts, and that inability to do the same in others is in some degree a crime which ought to be punished by suffering. They invent every possible excuse for withholding their demanded aid. But we can not hide ourselves from our own flesh and blood without sin. The Christian lives to bless his family and his home, to aid and comfort his poorer relatives and neighbors, to sanctify and teach his city and neighborhood, to exalt and improve his country and nation. All these are parts of his domestic, christian love, and fruits of the patriotic spirit which should adorn and dignify his religious character. And whatever toil or effort, or exposure within his reach may be required to save and bless others in his family or country will be cheerfully devoted to this great and useful purpose. Thus Esther realized and acknowledged her appointed duty and her designated time, and gave herself cheerfully to the work of mercy for her people.

Fourth. The time displayed her entire disinterestedness of spirit, and her trust in God. She resolved to put the request of Mordecai into immediate operation. Mere self-indulgence would have delighted in her own state of luxury and enjoyment, and have shut her ears and her heart against the cries and woes of her people. To preserve this people, she must hazard her own life. The king's law was peremptory and unyielding. If God should not be pleased to move the heart of the king, she must die for her temerity. But her mind was resolved to bear the whole hazard. She acknowledges in it the very purpose for which God has called her to her strange position. She will risk every thing to attain her end, even if she perish in the attempt. We can not now follow her in the experiment which she makes. But we hear her earnest spirit speaking out, "If I perish, I perish." "For how can I endure to see the evil which shall come unto my people, or how can I endure to see the destruction of my kindred?" And in this earnestness of consecration, she throws herself into the responsibility and the hazard of the undertaking.

Beautiful is this illustration of a disinterested and devoted spirit. I am content to perish to gain the great end of blessing to others which I have before me. Such was the love of our divine Redeemer for us. "For the joy that was set before him, he endured the cross and despised the shame." "He gave himself to die for us, a sacrifice for sin." "Herein was love." Such ought to be our love for Christ, willingly giving up ourselves to his service to glorify him in the way of his appointment, and to lay down our lives for his glory, and in the defense of his gospel. Such ought to be also our self-renouncing confidence in Christ, casting ourselves at his feet without doubt or fear. He graciously invites us and bids us come to him, to tell him of all our sins and wants. Let us learn to believe his sacred word. In entire trust, let us cast ourselves upon him, in affectionate faith leave all our wants in his hands, in humble hope expect his mercy and acceptance, content to perish if he be not true. He delights in those who thus truly honor him by believing his word and resting their hope upon that word. He will keep them in perfect peace whose hearts are stayed on him, because they trust in him. There let us fly for hope and refuge.

> "I can but perish if I go;
> I am resolved to try;
> For if I stay away, I know
> I shall for ever die."

XV.

Difficulties Cleared Up.

*"The king's heart is in the hands of the Lord; as the rivers of water he turneth it whithersoever he will."—*Proverbs*, xxi. 1.

The care of a gracious providence over a child of God, we have traced up to this point. And here a difficulty intervenes which she has no power to remove. The heart of the king himself must be directed and governed for her success in the purpose which she has formed. The difficulty of controlling the human heart God teaches us by a very striking comparison. "Will ye not tremble at my presence, which have placed the sand for the bound of the sea by a perpetual decree, that it can not pass it? and though the waves thereof toss themselves, yet can they not prevail; though they roar, yet can they not pass over it. But this people hath a revolting and rebellious heart; they are revolted and gone." (Jeremiah, v. 22.) Is it easier to command and govern the sea than to control a sinful human heart? So the Lord presents the subject. But yet the power that controls the one can also govern the other, and that as easily as a new channel may be given to the river in its downward course. So our text declares.

Esther's love and faith have been tried by peculiar difficulties. We have seen the time of great trial for her nation. They were sold to bondage and death. It was a time of great distress for Mordecai. His own death and the murder of hundreds of his countrymen seemed immediately before him. At such a time this captive orphan was brought to the throne. Her love for Mordecai, her interest in the welfare of her people, her disinterestedness in their protection and defense, have proved equal to the emergency in which her spirit is tried.

But why was all this display of excellence of character and fidelity to duty in Esther? We must not give the glory to her. This is the work of grace in a child of God. Her heart also is in the hands of the Lord, and it was he who moved, guided, and supported her in the crisis in which she was placed. She was made to feel that she had been brought to the kingdom for such a time as this, and she was enabled faithfully to fulfill her obligation to her time. Thus in this chamber of instruction do we see the Spirit working with the providence of God, and "whithersoever the Spirit was to go, thither were the wheels to go also." This is true piety under the divine Providence in a state of influence and exaltation. But there is now another heart to be moved, and a further display of the perfection and completeness which marks all the plans of the Most High. This we have now to consider.

First, Esther's heart was moved not to shrink from manifest duty. When her way was made clear to her own view, she immediately determined to pursue the path which seemed to be opened before her. Her duty might be extremely difficult, costly, dangerous to herself. But she embraced its call without hesitation or fear. All its hazards she could not know, some of them were perfectly apparent. And whatever they might be, she shrunk from nothing to which the will of God appeared to call her.

This is a most important element of true religion. "Add to your faith, virtue," courage, a manly and determined purpose to carry out its calls to their utmost extent. Stop not to ask leave of circumstances of personal convenience or indolent self-indulgence. But go forward in your appointed work. "It is not necessary that I should live, but it is necessary that I should go," has true heroism said with Luther in every age. Many an occasion of important usefulness we lose from fear of the hazard which may be involved, or from doubts of the results to which we may be brought. While we deliberate and question, our golden opportunity passes. "Enlargement and deliverance arise from some other quarter," and we lose all the privilege of the work, and all the blessings of the result. "I will go in unto the king," says Esther, "which is not according to law, and if I perish, I perish." It was a violation of form, but a fulfillment of duty. "To obey is better than sacrifice." "What man shall there be among you that shall have one sheep, and if it fall into a pit on the Sabbath day, will he not lay hold on it and lift it out?" This is a most important principle of human duty. That which is merely positive and formal in man's obligations must always give way to that which is moral and right in itself. The Sabbath was to be observed in worship, but not so as to involve the suffering or injury even of brute animals for the sake of it. Gifts are to be put into the Lord's treasury, but not so that parents in poverty were to be neglected or the needy and suffering refused. "These things ought ye to have done, and not to leave the others undone."

In the Church of England, in the end of the seventeenth century, a proposition was made for a collection in the churches for the French Protestants. Bishop Beveridge objected to it that it was in violation of the rubrics. Archbishop Tillotson replied, "Ah my lord, charity is higher than the rubrics." Duty is higher than forms.

Esther assumed all the hazard of formal irregularity, and all the possible danger of personal fidelity, and threw herself into the claims of personal duty as the crisis came. "If I perish, I perish." The example is of vast worth to us. How prone we are to shrink from disagreeable or dangerous duty. How many excuses we are able to frame for our neglect. How easy it becomes to satisfy our sinful hearts that God will not require that which it is so difficult or so dangerous to perform. Let me beg you, my young friends, to shun and resist this temptation to negligence and self-indulgence. Fly from no duty when the word and providence of God call you forward. Go on, and trust yourself to God, in a certain faith that he can and will order and prosper your goings in his way, for entire success to you and for glory to himself. He can make a little that a righteous man hath, better than great riches of the ungodly.

Second, Esther's heart was moved to sincere dependence on God. Habitually, the more bold and faithful is the Christian mind in duty, the more simple and entire is it in its conscious dependence and the exercise of its prayer and trust. First of all, this faithful child of God looks up to her Father in heaven. Her next message to Mordecai is, "Go, gather together all the Jews that are present in Shushan, and fast ye for me, and neither eat nor drink three days, night or day; and I also and my maidens will fast likewise—and *so* will I go in unto the king." So will she go, "strong in the Lord and in the power of his might." Fasting and prayer were a familiar exercise to believing Israelites. And while they united to lift up their hearts to the God of their salvation, she also would hold her assembly for united supplication in her own chamber, with her maidens, to whom already she had taught the habit of prayer and the presence and authority of God. God alone could arrest the calamity they feared. Her life and her hopes were wholly in his hands. And to him was her supplication made, for his protection and blessing in the hour of danger.

What a blessed example is this! How mighty and prevailing is the power of prayer! While Moses prayed, Israel prevailed over Amalek; while Moses prayed, the judgments of the Lord were averted from Israel. The whole history in the Scripture, and of all the church of God beyond the Scripture, is full of testimonies and illustrations of this power of real and earnest prayer. The promises of God abound upon this subject. "Ask and it shall be given unto you; seek and ye shall find; knock and it shall be opened unto you. For every one that asketh receiveth; and he that seeketh findeth; and to him that knocketh it shall be opened." "If two of you shall agree on earth, as touching any thing that they shall ask, it shall be done for them of my Father which is in heaven." You can never be overcome by any enemies, or overwhelmed by any dangers, if you commit all your ways unto the Lord. Begin every undertaking in life with prayer. Make God your constant counsellor, and while he thus leads you to prayer, he will open the way for you to an abundant blessing.

How happy for us all is this habit of prayer! The spirit of prayer is in itself a blessing to the soul, the spirit of peace. We pray, and our prayer returneth into our own bosom. God, who by his Holy Spirit bestows upon us this habit, presents one of his most precious gifts in this. Prayer seems the natural voice of danger and sorrow. The ancient philosopher said, "If a man would learn to pray, let him go to sea." The hour of the tempest will be to multitudes a new lesson in their relations to God. When men are in affliction and trouble they are easily led to cry unto God. But how beautiful and attractive is this habit of prayer in youth, in prosperity, in the hour of earthly joy! Then to make God our chief joy, and to tell him of all our gratitude and love towards him for his boundless mercies, is a privilege and delight indeed. Surely those of you who are happy and prosperous should pray. "The voice of joy and praise is in the tabernacles of the righteous." The wrath of God is poured upon the families that call not upon his name.

Esther and her maidens prayed. What if the husband do not or will not bless his household? Can not the mother and the wife collect her children and her maidens for prayer? How well I knew a blessed illustration of this. I had a friend, a man of wealth and hospitality, but a reckless, ungodly man. His house was filled with drinking companions like himself.

Gambling and riot made their abode beneath his roof and fattened upon his inherited wealth. His wife was a faithful, earnest Christian, who mourned in secret over her husband's sins, and labored to bring up her children in the fear and love of God. In constant, earnest prayer she told her troubles to the Lord of all, and poured forth her sorrows at his feet. On one occasion when a drunken party filled the house, she took her little ones and retired to her room and locked herself within. The liquor all exhausted, and the servants refused admission to her chamber, in the late hour of the night the drunken husband forced the door of her retirement. He started to find her on her knees in the midst of her children. Still more to hear his own name on her lips in the prayer she was at that moment offering. He stopped, and in a moment, in perfect silence, he crept to her side and knelt down upon the floor. She felt that he was there, but continued her supplication. The Lord heard that prayer. The man rose from his knees with new resolutions and purposes. He pledged himself to the Lord his

God, and to his own faithful wife, that he would from that hour seek and serve the Lord. He did so. For years I knew him, to the Saviour a most devoted, humble disciple, to me, a most affectionate, faithful friend. Long since have they both departed, gathered as a shock of corn cometh in his season, mature in grace. What a recompense to the long-tried fidelity of a faithful, praying wife! Can not the wife, the mother, pray with her children, her maidens, though the husband and the father will not? Thus Esther's example teaches us a lesson which would be inestimable and cheap, if it cost the whole of life to learn it.

Third. The king's heart was moved to listen and to accept her. Her three days of fasting and prayer had been accomplished. And "it came to pass, on the third day, that Esther put on her royal apparel, and stood in the inner court of the king's house; and the king sat upon his royal throne in the royal house, over against the gate of the house." Thus the believing, praying child of God presented herself before the earthly throne on which every thing for her poor heart depended, not knowing what might befall her there. But she went armed by faith, and strengthened by prayer, and God gave her the full blessing which she asked. "It was so, when the king saw Esther, the queen, standing in the court, that she obtained favor in his sight. And the king held out to Esther the golden scepter that was in his hand. So Esther drew near and touched the top of the scepter." Now her utmost fears are removed. The clouds have passed, and the Lord whom she loved has given her a token for good. This is the power of prayer, the work of providence, the influence of grace. The king's heart is in the hands of the Lord, and as the rivers of water, he has turned it according to his will. The king's bounty is overflowing. Whatever she desires, she may have. "Then said the king unto her, What wilt thou, Queen Esther? and what is thy request? It shall be given thee, to the half of the kingdom."

What a lesson in providence is this! The same power which leads to prayer, and supports us in prayer, at the same time works over other minds and other things to make an answer completely ready for our enjoyment. Thus said the angel to Daniel, "O, Daniel, a man greatly beloved, fear not—for from the first day that thou didst set thine heart to understand, and to chasten thyself before thy God, thy words were heard, and I am come for thy words." And thus Daniel himself testifies: "Whiles I was speaking in prayer, lo, the man Gabriel, whom I had seen in the vision at the beginning, being caused to fly swiftly, touched me; and he informed me, and talked with me, and said, At the beginning of thy supplications the commandment came forth, and I am come to show thee, for thou art greatly beloved."

How easily can God remove all the stumbling-blocks out of the way of his children. "What art thou, O, great mountain? Before Zerubbabel thou shalt become a plain." When we press on faithfully in the path of duty, all our mountains become a plain. Anticipated difficulties suddenly vanish; enemies whom we had expected are not found; the things which apparently threatened our hurt turn out to our advantage; and blessings which we had not dared to hope for crowd around our path. Thus Paul found it at Rome. He had many dangers and evils to fear in his captivity. But he testifies as the result, "The things which have happened unto me have fallen out rather unto the furtherance of the gospel, so that every way Christ is preached, and I therein do rejoice, yea, and will rejoice." Take this as one of your noble principles of christian conduct, my dear young friends. Fear no evils which threaten you in the path of duty. God will make your way plain and safe while you are doing his work and his will. Learn to say, like the holy Paul, "None of these things move me; neither count I my life dear unto myself, so that I may finish my course with joy, and the ministry which I have received of the Lord Jesus, to testify the gospel of the grace of God." Thus by prayer believing, by fidelity persevering, you will be made more than conquerors through Christ Jesus.

Fourth, God moved Esther's heart to great wisdom and prudence in her management of the undertaking she had assumed. The Spirit of the Almighty giveth man wisdom, and opens to him the way of understanding. Peculiar wisdom and skill often are imparted to us in answer to prayers for the accomplishment of the work of the Lord. Esther found it so. She does not at once declare her purpose to the king. She simply said, "If it seem good unto the king, let the king and Haman come this day unto the banquet that I have prepared for him." And when this step was finished, and at her banquet the king repeats the question, "What is thy petition? and it shall be granted thee; and what is thy request? even to the half of the kingdom it shall be performed," she replies by only asking a repetition of the king's visit. "My petition and my request is, if I have found favor in the sight of the king, and if it please the king to grant my petition, and to perform my request, let the king and Haman come to the banquet that I shall prepare for them, and I will do to-morrow as the king hath said."

There was here another wonderful interposition of the divine providence, which brought out Mordecai's merit and exaltation between these two banquets, to which we shall refer in its proper place. But Esther's wisdom is alone before us now. At the second banquet, "the king said again unto Esther, What is thy petition, Queen Esther? and it shall be granted thee; and what is thy request? and it shall be performed, even to the half of the kingdom." "Then Esther the queen answered and said, If I have found favor in thy sight O king, and if it please the king, let my life be given me at my petition, and my people at my request." Was there ever a cause more wisely managed! or more effectively and tenderly presented and argued!

But thus, the heart is in the hands of the Lord. It is he that giveth man wisdom. "The preparation of the heart in man and the answer of the tongue is from the Lord." Our dependence and prayer have no tendency to make us headlong or rash. We are still to prove, that "wisdom dwells with prudence, to find out knowledge of witty inventions." We are still to employ all the proper means and agencies which our utmost wisdom will suggest to attain the end we have in view. We ask our gracious God for his guidance and blessing, and then we go forward to our appointed work with simple trust in him, not knowing which shall prosper, whether this or that, but knowing that all things must work together for good to those who love him. He alone can prosper the work of our hands; but he can do it according to his own will, and will do it in his own way, and we look to him. True piety in the exercise of its faith and love and hope towards God, is the highest wisdom. It unites all the wisest calculation and effort of man with all the goodness and power of God. It is a fellowship, a partnership with God, in which he furnishes all the capital, and employs our sanctified labors alone; in which we strive to be faithful, and he promises to bless.

This blessed path of duty is ever open to you. In one great question before the King of kings, you can never doubt the path of obligation or expediency. The Lord your Saviour requires your heart's devotion to him. He demands the consecration of your life to him. He sits upon the throne of grace before you, exalted to be a prince and Saviour, to give repentance and forgiveness of sins to all who come into his courts. Why withhold from him the offering he seeks? He bids you come with all boldness to his feet. He encourages you to offer your petition and request. He assures you he is more ready to hear than you are to pray, and is willing to give you far more than you desire or deserve. Go to him without fear. Trust his accepting love without a doubt. He will stretch forth the scepter of his pardon and welcome. He will meet you in the overflowing of his mercy and compassion. He will give you his own kingdom, even life eternal. Go, try him. Try his word. Try his power. Try his promise. Every time is the acceptable time, when your heart is truly ready to go. Every day is the day of salvation, when your soul really seeks it. Make the experiment then for yourselves. And see how soon the darkness will pass, your fears be forgotten, your sorrows be turned within you, and your whole souls shall rejoice in an accepting, all-sufficient Saviour, with joy unspeakable and full of glory.

XVI.

The Righteous Ruler.

"When the righteous are in authority, the people rejoice."—Proverbs, xxix. 2.

This is the position occupied by Esther in our present contemplation. She is exalted to great authority. The Jewish orphan has become not only the Queen of Persia, but also a ruling favorite with the king, and supreme in power by his authority. Her petition and her request have been granted even to the half of the kingdom.

The purity and excellence of her own character have shined before us. The wisdom of her management in the crisis through which she has passed, we have partly seen. But this needs to be more particularly considered. Her argument with the king in behalf of her petition was as remarkable for its wisdom, as her manner of arranging the negotiation.

At the second banquet, she openly and affectionately declares her suit. "Let my life be given me at my petition, and my people at my request." She had found the appropriate time for her request, and her words were most fitly spoken, "like apples of gold in a network of silver." The king, amazed, listens to her earnest and ingenuous plea.

She presents the extreme cruelty of the persecution from which she begs relief. "For we are sold, I and my people, to be destroyed and to perish." Innocent and helpless, under a false accusation, to glut the revenge and pacify the envy of a single oppressor, they were sold by the king himself to the destroyer. Such a proceeding could never be consistent with the character or government of a righteous king. A sorrow like this compelled her to speak. If the evil had been less, "if we had been sold for bondmen and bondwomen, I had held my tongue." Patiently and quietly she would have endured this lesser trial. But this causeless death decreed on all her nation compelled her to complain. The king listened with surprise and self-condemnation.

She proceeded to display the folly of such a persecution. "The enemy could not countervail the king's damage." He could in no way compensate for the loss of multitudes of industrious and useful people, thus cruelly murdered. Whatsoever sum he might agree to pay the loss to the king and the empire would be immense. And why should the king endure all this loss, and bear the responsibility of all this cruelty, to gratify the malice of a single oppressor? This could be no evidence of wisdom in him, and no increase of glory to his government.

Esther's wisdom and earnestness were made effectual. The hand of the Lord turned the king's heart. "Who is he?" he exclaims, "and where is he, that durst presume in his heart to do so?" Esther sees her success complete, and proceeds to tell the story of her wrongs. The succeeding incidents come up again for our contemplation. The result was the overturning of Haman's plot, the giving to Esther the house of Haman, and her complete exaltation to power as the deliverer and ruler of her people.

Thus is she brought out in a full trial and

proof of her fidelity in duty to God, and the Lord's fidelity in promise to her. How beautifully have all her virtues been displayed. How completely has she justified the grace which had set her up on high. When such an one is raised to authority the people rejoice in her exaltation. Every one is ready to say she deserves to reign. They rejoice in the results of her exaltation. Abounding blessings come upon them from her dominion. And we have now to trace some of the advantages which arose from Esther's power.

First, Mordecai rejoices. Much as his lone heart had grieved over her separation from him, now he sees in the end how gracious the Lord is. His hidden myrtle blooms in open sight, perfect in beauty and clothed with blessings for the refreshment of the multitudes of her people. Esther's first step in power is to acknowledge and exalt Mordecai. She announces to the king who he is, and "what he was unto her." She gave to Mordecai the house of Haman, and the king took off his ring which he had given to Haman and gave it to Mordecai.

How beautiful and exemplary is this exhibition of Esther's affectionate and grateful heart! This is true religion in one of its loveliest fruits. Mordecai may be poor, uneducated, perhaps unattractive in aspect. Mere worldly wealth and elevation desires rather to forget than to acknowledge such relations, and shuns the renewal of an intimacy which may furnish no outward credit. But Esther's mind is elevated far above that low and selfish platform. She delights to proclaim her obligations to Mordecai, " what he was unto her." One of the most precious personal elements of her new power, in her view, was the ability which it gave her to be useful to him. It is a noble spirit; and when prosperity thus crowns a filial, grateful, dutiful temper in a child, the joy which it imparts has no limit, but in the acquaintance which others may have with the story of the excellence from which it flows. Take it as an example, and if God shall ever crown your earthly labors with wealth and power, delight to employ them to increase the happiness of those who have known and loved you when you were young and poor.

Second. The Jews in Persia rejoice. The

decree has been issued for their destruction. Letters sealed with the king's ring had been sent to "the king's lieutenants, and to the governors that were over every province, and to the rulers of every people of every province, in the name of King Ahasuerus, to destroy, to kill, and to cause to perish all Jews, both young and old, little children and women, in one day, and to take the spoil of them for a prey." Never was a more terrific order issued by authority of man, or with more apparent indifference. "The king and Haman sat down to drink, but the city of Shushan was perplexed."

The day was fixed on which this fearful destruction was to be accomplished, and that appointed time was now rapidly approaching. The decree could not be recalled, either in the time allowed, or according to the unchangeable authority of the royal law. Fearful as it was, it appeared inevitable and must be executed. This perplexing crisis Esther was to meet. Again she "came before the king, and fell down at his feet, and besought him with tears to put away the mischief of Haman, and his device that he had devised against the Jews." She entreated him that a decree might be "written to reverse the letters devised by Haman." "For how," she exclaimed in the earnestness of her soul, "how can I endure to see the evil that shall come unto my people? or how can I endure to see the destruction of my kindred?"

The decree could not be reversed. But the king would give to Mordecai unlimited authority in the case, to do all that could be done consistent with this unchanging rule of Persia. "Write ye also for the Jews as it liketh you, in the king's name, and seal it with the king's ring; for the writing which is written in the king's name, and sealed with the king's ring, may no man reverse." This Mordecai could do, and this he did. He wrote unto the Jews, in all the hundred twenty and seven provinces, letters, "wherein the king granted the Jews, who were in every city, to gather themselves together, and to stand for their life, to destroy, to slay, and to cause to perish all the power of the people and province that would assault them, and to take the spoil of them for a prey." This new decree would give them the royal protection in defending themselves. None but the bitterest of their enemies would be willing to persevere in their projected destruction against the will of the king. Against such their own power of defense would be sufficient.

The decree for their protection was sent forth with the utmost speed. And "Mordecai went out from the presence of the king in royal apparel, and the city of Shushan rejoiced and was glad." "The Jews had light and gladness and joy and honor; and in every province and in every city, whithersoever the king's commandment and his decree came, the Jews had joy and gladness and a feast and a good day. And many of the people of the land became Jews; for the fear of the Jews fell upon them."

This was the rejoicing in the righteous authority of Esther. The star of Persia was shining with a new brightness upon her people. Many hearts were engaged in praising God for such a ruler, and in earnest gratitude to Esther for such protection. David had said, "a just ruler over men, ruling in the fear of God, shall be as the light of the morning when the sun riseth, even a morning without clouds." Such did Esther prove to be to her people. She scattered blessings upon them all, and many rejoiced under her wise government and care.

Third, distant Jews rejoiced also in the results of her exaltation. She was raised up to be not only a protector to her people in Persia, but to be their restorer also in their father's land. By her influence blessings were poured upon the nation who had returned to Palestine, and messengers of glad tidings were sent to them. This is a most interesting view of her appointed work. By her influence probably, Ezra, the famous scribe of Israel, was commissioned to gather and restore the people in their own land.

The whole nation of Israel was still under the dominion of the King of Persia. Palestine was a province of his kingdom. Seventy years before Esther's time, Cyrus had given liberty to the Jews to return to their own land, and they had done something towards the restoration of their habitations and their city. The first six chapters of Ezra give us a history of this return, and of the many difficulties and trials they encountered in their work of national restoration. They had labored on in the midst of great hostility from the surrounding heathen, and of great affliction from their own poverty.

But now there is an influence in Persia which works for the protection and prosperity of Israel. Esther has been raised up to be the mother of her people, and the king her husband is taught by her influence to be their friend and a blessing to them. "The king's heart is in the hands of the Lord." With what delight do we read in this connection the story of Ezra, and the decree of the king giving him permission to return to Palestine, in the seventh chapter of his book. "This Ezra went up from Babylon; and he was a ready scribe in the law of Moses, which the Lord God of Israel had given; and the king granted him all his request, according to the hand of the Lord his God upon him. For Ezra had prepared his heart to seek the law of the Lord, and to do it, and to teach Israel statutes and judgments."

Listen to the decree from the **King of Persia**

which Ezra was commissioned to bear with him to Palestine: "Artaxerxes, king of kings, unto Ezra the priest, the scribe of the law of the God of heaven, perfect peace. I make a decree that all they of the people of Israel, which are minded of their own free will to go up to Jerusalem, go with thee. Whatsoever is commanded by the God of heaven, let it be diligently done for the house of the God of heaven; and thou Ezra, after the wisdom of thy God that is in thine hand, set magistrates that they may judge the people, all such as know the laws of thy God, and teach ye them that know them not."

Thus this Persian king wrote in the seventh year of his reign, three years, perhaps, after Esther had come to the royal state as his queen. Well did Ezra reply, in the gratitude of his heart, "Blessed be the Lord God of our fathers, who hath put such a thing as this in the king's heart, and hath extended mercy to me before the king; and I was strengthened as the hand of the Lord my God was upon me." What a blessing it must be to man, when earthly rulers take this high and religious ground! What a surprise would it be in this Christian land, if such a message should come from the chief magistrate to the people! But why should this not be always the rule and style of language and action with the governors of men? Ought rulers to be ashamed of acknowledging openly the great Ruler of all? Ought they not always to adopt the word and will of God as their guide, and thus rule over men in his fear? Blessed will be that coming day, so surely promised, when "the kingdoms of this world shall become the kingdoms of our Lord and of his Christ." Never does an earthly ruler seem so exalted and great, and never is he, or can he be, so useful and acceptable to men, as when he seeks only the glory of this great King of kings. We may hardly speak of the King of Persia as such. But this decree was probably the result of Esther's influence and the proof of her power. She thus became a mother to her people, and her nation in their distant land rejoiced in the authority with which she was clothed. "When the righteous are in authority, the people rejoice."

Fourth. After this mission of Ezra, we find

Esther's influence prevailing still, and other portions of her nation made to rejoice in her authority. Ezra finished his work; he established the Lord's worship in Jerusalem; he gathered and prepared the sacred books of Scripture which God had given to his people; and his name has been held in grateful and honored remembrance, as a restorer to his downcast nation. But some twelve years after, we find the Jews still exalted, and a godly, praying Jew appointed to the responsible office of cupbearer of the King of Persia. And there is further joy among the people under Esther's authority.

You have the interesting history of this subsequent blessing in the story of Nehemiah. In the twentieth year of Ahasuerus some of Nehemiah's brethren came back from Jerusalem, and gave him mournful accounts of the sufferings of the Israelites in Palestine. They were in great affliction and reproach. The wall of Jerusalem was broken down, and the gates thereof were burned with fire. His heart was filled with grief at this intelligence. He sat down and wept, and mourned certain days, and fasted and prayed before the God of heaven. He acknowledged the sins of his people, but pleaded the promises and covenant of the Lord for them, and especially asked for guidance and direction for himself in such a crisis. "O Lord," he said, "I beseech thee, let now thine ear be attentive to the prayer of thy servant, and prosper, I pray thee, thy servant this day, and grant him mercy in the sight of this man." He was the king's cupbearer. On that day he took the wine as usual, and gave it unto the king. But his own heart and countenance were sad, and he could not conceal his grief.

The king perceived his sorrow, and kindly said to him, "Why is thy countenance sad, seeing thou art not sick? This is nothing else but sorrow of heart." He was filled with fear at this unusual demand, and in his secret heart he "prayed unto the God of heaven." The queen was sitting by the side of the king, and Nehemiah told them of his mournful intelligence from Jerusalem and his own earnest desire to go and aid the oppressed people by his own personal effort and countenance. The king gave him permission, and "he set him a time" for his return. The subsequent history of Nehemiah shows the value and the usefulness of his mission.

But the whole story remarkably displays to us the power of prayer, of secret inward prayer. This lifting up of the heart to God is a delightful exercise and an instrument of peculiar power. A particular friend of mine was required to pass through a terrible surgical operation, which endured for near an hour, before any of the modern agencies of alleviation had been discovered. I asked him how he could endure such continued suffering. His answer was, "I was praying earnestly all the time, and somehow I hardly felt it. My Saviour seemed to take the pain almost entirely away." Thus God will hear this fervent, inwrought prayer, prayer which may be made at all times and in all places. Thus God will bless those who call upon him. Nehemiah found it so, Esther found it so. You will always find it so when you call upon God in truth, and with a pure heart fervently. The answer to Nehemiah's prayer you may trace in all the succeeding history of his usefulness to his people, and in all the influence which Esther continued to exercise over them. But he was not the only praying soul among the people. We have traced the effectual operations of prayer through the whole history. We may trace it still. God made Esther a blessing in answer to the prayers of his people, and her people and her father's land rejoiced in a prayer-hearing and prayer-answering God.

Fifth. Beyond even Ezra and Nehemiah and the Jews of Persia and Palestine, Esther's rule gave joy to Israel. The nation still maintain their annual commemorative festival in honor of Esther, in every land. It is the last festival of their year. The feast of Passover begins their year in the first month, and the feast of Purim, or Esther, closes it in the twelfth. So we read in the conclusion of this story, "The Jews ordained and took upon them, and upon their seed, and upon all such as joined themselves unto them, that these days should be kept throughout every generation, every family, every province and every city; and that these days of Purim should not fail from among the Jews, nor the memorial of them perish from their seed." Thus the righteous is in everlasting remembrance, and multitudes rejoice when the righteous rule. Generations rise up to call them blessed. The captive orphan of Shushan has never been forgotten, and can never be. The righteous Queen of Persia abides and will abide in the grateful memory of her people. Little could she have imagined what the God of her fathers designed to do with her. She yielded to his will; she obeyed his commands; she sought his guidance; she trusted in his protection and promise; and he made her an everlasting blessing to multitudes of her nation, and a lovely pattern of conduct and character to his whole family on earth.

This is the illustration of true piety, in the prosperity which attends it. This is our second lesson in the great school of providence. This is the second chamber of instruction in the book of Esther, and the second of those great pictures of human history which it contains. We have seen the selected instance of true piety beginning in the lowest stage of human life and closing in the highest; starting in its course in obscurity and human neglect, finishing it in permanent and enlarged usefulness, amidst the homage and applause of mankind. This must always be its course and the rule of its history.

God may not be pleased to exalt all to the same outward glory. But the principle of protection and prosperity, for all his people, is the same. He will surely make them useful, and a blessing in the earth—how extensively or how permanently they can never tell. He gives them opportunity and means to enlarge the joys of their fellow-men; he adorns their own walk in life with beauty and peace; he crowns their memory with gratitude and honor.

All this has been illustrated for us in the history of Esther, which becomes both a type and a pledge of similar government and similar results of blessing for all the children of God. There is, in a far higher sense, a crown and a throne for all. There comes a day of exaltation, when all who love God shall meet around that throne of glory in everlasting triumph. Is it not a wise and happy choice, to have the Lord of hosts upon your side? Is it not a reasonable, profitable choice, to make his ways your ways, and his will your will, in every thing? Is it not a blessed portion to be found cleansed by him from every stain, and renewed by him in every decay—washed in the atoning blood of a glorious Saviour—created in holiness by the life-giving power of his Holy Spirit? Every step in this path is an upward step to glory. Every day in its history brings the fullness of glory still nearer to the redeemed soul.

My young friends, are you not willing to enter upon this path, and faithfully pursue it? Are you not willing to take the Lord for your God, the Saviour of Israel for your Saviour? What does he ask of you but to believe his word, to choose his service, to make him your ruler and guide, to seek his Spirit and obey his commands? This is a simple, but a happy path for life. It is the way of peace, the way to glory. Let me entreat you to choose it as your own, and to walk therein faithfully for ever.

XVII

Vain Prosperity.

"I was envious at the foolish, when I saw the prosperity of the wicked. Behold, these are the ungodly who prosper in the world."—Psalm lxxiii. 3, 12.

Two great lessons of divine providence we have already studied in the book of Esther. The world has displayed its emptiness in the history of Ahasuerus, and true religion has exhibited its happiness and security in the story of Esther. We come now to a new scene and a new lesson. We pass into the third chamber of instruction which the divine government has arranged for us. It is the chamber of human crime, of the wickedness of man; and we shall see how human wickedness is made to demonstrate its folly in the course of Haman.

This is a most important line of divine teaching. As surely as worldly indulgence results in disappointment and vanity, and true piety issues in security, exaltation and peace, under the constant providence of God, does human wickedness, however crafty and well arranged, involve its agents in confusion and overthrow at last. "Fools make a mock at sin." Illustrations of such folly are constantly recurring. The wicked may appear to prosper and triumph for a season. They may seem to increase in riches. They are not in trouble as other men. Pride compasseth them about as a chain, violence covereth them as a garment. Their wealth increases in their hands, they have more than heart could wish. By such apparent temporary prosperity they are led on to the utmost rebellion against God, and to entire confidence in their own success. "They set their mouth against the heavens." They "make a mock at sin." "They say, How doth God know? and is there knowledge in the Most High."

The servants of God may be sometimes so foolish as to envy the prosperity of the wicked, and so rebellious as to charge God with want of kindness and protection to his own children, so that they "have cleansed their hearts in vain, and washed their hands in innocency."

For they seem to be plagued all day long and chastened every morning. But how temporary is this delusion. A little time unravels the whole apparent mystery and demonstrates the faithfulness and goodness of God, and the wisdom of those who choose and love him. The seventy-third Psalm is a comment on this whole discussion and scheme of thought, wonderfully accurate and striking. It displays the habitual system and result of the divine vindication. God does not visit the ungodly always with direct and dreadful judgments. The earth does not open for their destruction. The mountains do not flame upon them. The lightnings do not strike them. They seem to themselves perfectly secure, because not immediately punished.

But a sure result is before them, and in due time their sin finds them out. They are taken in their own craftiness. They are set in slippery places. They are cast down into destruction and brought into desolation as in a moment. They prepare the discovery and the ruin for themselves, so that their own prosperity destroys them, and when they are destroyed, they find that they have but eaten of the fruit of their own doings. As a dream when one awaketh, so does their image vanish and become despised.

This is our third lesson in this school of providence. We see here the most crafty and accomplished wickedness caught in its own snare, and made the instrument of its own punishment. All its schemes of evil are overruled; all its revengeful and hostile purposes are made to bless those against whom they have been prepared. It falls into the very pit it has digged for another. And God is vindicated in all the ways of his providence and government, while he brings out the sinner's condemnation and ruin from his own transgression. This is the important chapter of human history which we have now to contemplate.

The subject of this illustration is Haman, an Agagite, whom Ahasuerus "promoted and advanced, and set his seat above all the princes that were with him." He is made to test for us the folly of human crime, and to illustrate the certainty of the sinner's punishment under the providence of God. And we shall gain much instruction by faithfully tracing for ourselves the facts and warnings of his story.

First, we see every possible advantage of condition and power conceded to him. This has been the fact in each of the previous illustrations. God allows the cause opposed to him to have all the means of apparent triumph and success, so that if such opposition may ever prevail, it shall have the fullest opportunity. When he would show us the vanity of the world he allows it to heap up every possible means of gratification and pleasure. When he would show us the security of piety he permits every possible difficulty and objection to be in its way; so when he would show the folly and weakness of the sinner, he permits him to combine every thing on his side, which could operate to give success to his plans and assure the accomplishment of his wicked designs. Haman shall complain of no want on his side of any instrument which might render his triumph certain. And then in defiance of all his power and his craft, God will overturn all his schemes, and bring him to desolation as in a moment. The story of Haman's gains and advantages is most remarkable. Could the wickedness of man ever succeed, it must in circumstances like his.

He was rich; unlimited wealth seemed to be in his control. For a single grant of power, he offered the king ten thousand talents of silver, near twenty millions of dollars. The extent of this offer is enormous, and doubtless he hoped to gain much of it from the robbing of the Jews whom he would destroy. Yet even among the wealth of Persia, Haman was distinguished, boasting to his friends "of the glory of his riches." We need not stop to enlarge upon these elements of power. Not only rich, he was highly exalted in station. The king had given him the seat of honor next the throne, and had advanced him above all the princes and servants of the king. No subject of the monarch equaled him in rank, or in the influence which his station gave. Rich and exalted, he was powerful also. The king had given him his own ring, and had thus entrusted him with unlimited authority. "The writing which was written in the king's name and sealed with the king's ring, might no man reverse." All the powers of government in the kingdom were thus placed in the hands of Haman. In this high condition, he was flattered and honored by universal homage. "All the king's servants that were in the king's gate bowed and reverenced Haman, for the king had so commanded concerning him." And when the king asked, "What shall be done unto the man whom the king delighteth to honor?" Haman could imagine no rival to himself in Persia. And "Haman thought within his heart, to whom would the king delight to do honor more than to myself?"

Thus Haman seemed to stand on the very pinnacle of human greatness and prosperity. He "had more than heart could wish." There was nothing of the things of earth left to be desired. What means of enjoyment he had, if he sought his own pleasure. What opportunities of usefulness, if he desired to bless his fellow-men, were placed in his hands. Nothing was withheld from him. And as we survey his condition we exclaim, What gratitude such a man must owe to God! What blessings he might bestow upon his fellow-men. But Haman had no heart for gratitude, no love for mankind, no wish to be made a blessing to the world in which he lived. He was an enemy to God, to his people, and to his truth. The controlling spirit of his wicked heart was selfishness. His own apparent advantage and gain occupied all his thoughts and directed all his plans. The more he had the more his unsatisfied and covetous heart demanded still. And if in any thing he should be limited or opposed, the more grasping and intolerant would his selfish nature become. What a view this is of the wickedness of man! And yet illustrations of it constantly occur. Instead of finding man growing contented with abundance, and gaining in love to God and man, as he gains in the means of earthly prosperity, we see him habitually becoming more worldly, more exacting, and more covetous still. Not often are such elements of human advantage combined in the possession of any one man as we see here displayed. But God means to show us that no human power or prosperity can secure a certain triumph to the wickedness of man, and to manifest the unreasonable and sinful discontent of man amidst the utmost circumstances of prosperity. "Though hand join in hand the wicked shall not go unpunished."

Second, we see the small amount of Haman's alleged deficiencies. Every thing is subject to his control, and every person yields to him a willing reverence but one poor Jew who sat at the king's gate. "Mordecai bowed not nor did him reverence." The submission of all others was cheerful and entire. This single man refused the homage which he demanded and which the king ordained. How perfectly trifling the exception seemed. One more so we can hardly conceive. It probably would be impossible to array a state of earthly prosperity which should have in it less to annoy or to disturb than this. Millions of blessings and means of happiness freely bestowed. One single occasional annoyance interjected among them.

My dear young friends, what an illustration of the prosperity of this world. It is impossible that any earthly portion should be free from every cause of complaint. The decay and sorrow which human sin produces must everywhere in some shape be found. There is everywhere a crook in the lot, whatever the lot may be, some earthly sorrow left to mingle with the brightest collection of earthly joys. It is left as a token of God's authority, as a test of man's submission, as a teacher of contentment and humility in the midst of occasions for pride and self-indulgence. Earthly advantages and gains puff up the pride of the heart, and a condition without a cross would be a sure destruction. God, therefore, ever reserves one fact at least, withheld from man. There is to every man a Mordecai in the gate, an unbending and unsubmissive difficulty of some kind in human life, to guard the children of God from the ruin which prosperity would bring, and to awaken the sinful to a consciousness of the insufficiency of an earthly portion, and the importance of something higher and something better than earth can give. Less than Haman's sorrow no living man can have. Less ground of complaint in any earthly state no wicked man can ever find.

But this fact of trial in human condition is always a constantly recurring one. It was so here. Day by day Haman must pass the gate, and Mordecai could not be avoided. The sorrow is small but it is ever present, like a broken tooth, or a missing step in the stairs on which we must habitually pass. It can never be forgotten. A submissive mind receives it as a call for acknowledgment and humility. The little trial becomes a constant discipline and means of improvement. A rebellious mind makes it an occasion of complaint, and the same annoyance hardens the heart in rebellion and impiety. Let us make a friend and teacher of every Mordecai in our way. We shall never be without him. We may gain much from him. In Haman's case, what a blessing he might have been. In the midst of Haman's prosperity, it was a constant call for consideration, for repentance, for forbearance, for gratitude to God. But Haman's wicked heart could not so receive it. "When Haman saw that Mordecai bowed not nor did him reverence, then was Haman full of wrath."

Third, this leads us to mark the effect of this one exception upon Haman's feelings and mind. This single deficiency completely destroyed all his enjoyment and peace. What a commentary we have upon his condition and mind, v. 9: "Haman went forth that day joyful and with a glad heart, but when Haman saw Mordecai in the king's gate, that he stood not up, nor moved for him, he was full of indignation against Mordecai. And when he came home, he called for his friends, and Zeresh his wife; and Haman told them of the glory of his riches, and the multitude of his children, and all the things wherein the king had promoted him, and how he had advanced him above the princes and servants of the king. Haman said, moreover, Yea, Esther the queen did let no man come in with the king unto the banquet that she had prepared, but myself. Yet all this availeth me nothing so long as I see Mordecai the Jew sitting at the king's gate." Miserable man! All beside this one annoying fact was nothing. Property, power, friends, honor were nothing. One desire ungratified, one obstacle encountered, destroyed them all. This is the spirit of a wicked heart. Its rebellion is unconquered by the mercies it enjoys—all its blessings are forgotten in the one complaint of its deprivation. The language of repining is considered the utterance of just remonstrance.

An eminent and aged friend of mine in the ministry, who was a pattern of meekness and submission, was visited on one occasion by a neighbor of wealth and prosperity from whom a son had been taken by death. The visiter was in great distress. He had no language to utter but complaint. Every thing, he said, was gone from him. God had dealt most severely with him. No man appeared to him to have been so afflicted. The venerable minister heard him long in silence, and then replied, " God has taken from me six children in mature life, each of them as desirable and valuable as yours. But I feel no right and no disposition to complain. The Lord gave, and the Lord hath taken away. Blessed be the name of the Lord." The difference between the two in the goods of this world was great. But the difference which grace had made on the other side, was vastly greater.

To make a man happy whose heart is astray from God, is impossible. Whatever of earthly bounties may be given, there is the secret feeling of remorse and consciousness of guilt which nothing can silence or dismiss. The mind is in rebellion against the only power which can give it peace. How many hearts are there in this condition! The world is full of bounties for them. They sometimes appear to be happy; but their enjoyment is all a mask; their laughter is mad; their inward spirit is fretful, rebellious and unsatisfied; the thoughts are occupied with murmurings and complaints. This is a spirit which is to be guarded against in its very start. Allow it no existence, tolerate it not for a moment, contemplate your blessings abounding; look not at your deprivations; see what God has given you; think not of what he has been pleased to withhold. When the exception in your condition, whatever it may be, is forced upon your notice, make it the occasion of some new duty. Learn to yield your own will to the gracious will of God. Seek his Spirit to recall and subdue you, to establish the claims and the authority of conscience, and gratitude, and divine obligation in your heart. And let Mordecai remind you every day of the innumerable comforts you enjoy beside.

Fourth. All these circumstances in Haman's condition showed how small was his temptation to crime. God not only allowed every circumstance of advantage on his side to accomplish his wickedness, if he determined to pursue it, but made it also perfectly unreasonable and without excuse, by giving him no special temptation to his sin. So, you remember, Nathan is sent to reason with David upon the peculiar sinfulness of his crime, in this very connection. "There were two men in one city, the one rich, the other poor. The rich man had exceeding many flocks and herds; but the poor man had nothing save one little ewe lamb, which he had brought and nourished up; and it grew up together with him and with his children; it did eat of his own meat, and drank of his own cup, and lay in his bosom, and was unto him as a daughter. And there came a traveler unto the rich man, and he spared to take of his own flock and of his own herd, to dress for the wayfaring man that was come unto him, but took the poor man's lamb and dressed it for the man that was come to him." There was no excuse for such a crime. Accordingly, "David's anger was greatly kindled against the man, and he said to Nathan, As the Lord liveth, the man that has done this thing shall surely die."

Thus Haman had no reasonable excuse, no motive but in his own wicked heart, for the course of crime on which he was to enter. It was simply the working of malicious wickedness, his own fretful, hateful temper. Mordecai did him no injury, diminished none of his real advantages or possessions. The people of Mordecai were perfectly innocent of any crime in this relation. But Haman's indulgence of his own hostile and self-defending spirit, opened a way to wickedness which was enormous, almost inconceivable.

Such is the process of yielding to the suggestions and claims of a sinful temper. It leads us from one step to another in the course of sin, until the sinner is ensnared in unexpected guilt, and entangled in crimes hideous in their aspect, and beyond his power to escape. It may be the appetite for gain, the haste to be rich, which pushes him on to every sacrifice of duty, and through every species of fraud, and every scheme of attempted concealment, till God suddenly reveals the whole plot, and the man is ruined beyond recovery. It may be the dominion of lust which entices and entangles its victim, until completely involved in degradation or fear of revenge, with no apparent hope of escape, it forces the wretched culprit to murder and to suicide. It may be the excitement for revenge which plunges itself in blood, under the goading of its hateful power, and drives the guilty man on from crime to crime, till every thing for earth and for eternity has been sacrificed in his course of desperation and ruin.

Let no young man feel that he is safe from temptation to the worst of crimes in allowing the power for a moment of such a spirit.

Watch against its first encroachment. Cultivate, as the rule of life, high and pure motives, habits of self-control, refusal to receive affronts or to take offense at the errors or neglect of others. Above all, take to you the whole armor of God for your defense. Stand ever and wholly on the side of Christ, under the guidance and blessing of his Spirit continually sought. This is the only security, and from what evils and crimes it may deliver you, eternity alone can unfold.

XVIII.

Plotting in Vain.

"The wicked plotteth against the just, and gnasheth upon him with his teeth. The Lord shall laugh at him, for he seeth that his day is coming."—PSALM xxxvii. 12, 13.

THUS the divine Providence leads us on in an increasing knowledge of the vain attempts of the wicked. How little we can anticipate the plans of God! We often look at the present state of things as hopeless when they are nearest a remedy, often as satisfying when they are on the eve of an overthrow. We judge the Lord by feeble sense. But his ways and plans are fixed and established. He is the Lord, he changeth not. His ways are known unto him from the beginning, and his purposes travel on in a certain progress to their fixed conclusion. How important it is for us to remember this great truth. While he is perfectly tranquil in the knowledge of his own power and design, the heart that lives most by faith in him will be tranquil also, in the confidence with which it rests in both.

The illustration of Haman's history perfectly conforms to the text which we have set before us now. All his plotting against the just, and gnashing upon him with his teeth, came to nothing. The Lord derided his attempts and overthrew completely all his schemes. This we are now to see. Haman's character and the advantages of his condition have been before us, and we proceed to consider the scheme of destruction which he arranged with the utmost craft. It seemed in its arrangement perfectly secure. Its accomplishment appeared certain and beyond resistance.

First, Haman's malice was extreme, equal to any result to which it might lead. There was no reluctance, no holding back in the carrying out his purposes of wickedness to the utmost. It was religious hatred. They told him that Mordecai was a Jew. The idolatrous Agagite, like all the heathen, detested this people. All the principles of their faith and their worship were intolerant of his idolatry. Human hatred has hardly risen higher than in its manifestation against the Jews. And Haman rejoiced at an opportunity to bring destruction if possible upon them. It was personal indignation. Mordecai persisted in an open affront against himself. His station was despised, his wealth was disregarded, his power was not feared, and all this was by a Jew. Haman was full of wrath. He grasped the suggestion of his friends, " let a gallows be made of fifty cubits high, and speak thou unto the king that Mordecai may be hanged thereon." It was the hatred of conscious weakness. In the plan which he formed he could do nothing. He had no power to kill Mordecai, or to destroy his nation without the king's permission. And he hated them the more from his inability to accomplish his purposes of vengeance. His vengeance enlarged far beyond the original cause which excited it. " He thought scorn to lay hands on Mordecai alone, for they had showed him the people of Mordecai. Wherefore Haman sought to destroy all the Jews that were throughout the whole kingdom of Ahasuerus, even the people of Mordecai." This was a deep and dreadful vengeance indeed. But the malice of Haman was equal to it.

Yet how wonderful is the extent of human malice like this! It is impossible for man to say how far his heart shall go in the way of sin. "The heart is deceitful above all things and desperately wicked. Who can know it?" When man allows indulgence to its sinful purposes, he casts himself upon a current that knows no limits; it gathers strength as it rushes forward; it sweeps by at last, with no opportunity left for resistance or escape. The wise man avoids every exposure to the danger. "He that trusteth in his own heart is a fool." How Hazael illustrates this in his interview with Elisha (2 Kings, viii. 11): "Elisha settled his countenance upon him until he was ashamed. And the man of God wept. And Hazael said, Why weepeth my lord? And he answered, Because I know the evil thou wilt do to the children of Israel. Their strongholds wilt thou set on fire, and their young men wilt thou slay with the sword, and will dash their children, and rip up their women with child. And Hazael said, But what, is thy servant a dog, that he should do this great thing?" And yet he did all this, impossible as he imagined it to be. How little he understood his own heart, or the increasing power of indulged and growing sin.

Second, Haman's plan was extremely crafty and determined. It involved many successive steps, and he faithfully persevered through them all. He began by trying to secure a higher influence, as he supposed, to prosper his scheme. He cast lots to discover the best time to accomplish his plan. This was considered a direct appeal to the Deity. "The lot is cast into the lap; but the whole disposing thereof is of the Lord." But wicked men have adopted this as a plan of success or luck in every age and land. And Haman appeals to his idols for power to accomplish his plans of destruction upon the people of God. The disposing of his lot we shall hereafter see. Then Haman misrepresented the people, whom he would destroy, before the king. They were worthless; there was no profit in them; they were troublesome and offensive; their laws were diverse from his; they were rebellious; they would not keep the king's commandment; they were an injurious people, scattered everywhere among the subjects of the king, in all the provinces of the kingdom. Yet while he made all these accusations against the people, he did not designate them by name to the king. "And Haman said unto King Ahasuerus, There is a certain people scattered abroad and dispersed among the people, in all the provinces of thy kingdom; and their laws are diverse from all people; neither keep they the king's laws; therefore it is not for the king's profit to suffer them. If it please the king, let it be written that they may be destroyed." How malicious and wicked all this train of accusations was. Yet when the wicked heart of man is given up to a course of crime, nothing can be considered beyond its reach, in guilt. So desirous and determined is Haman for the destruction of the Jews, that he offers next an immense payment of money for the grant of power which he seeks. "I will pay ten thousand talents of silver to the hands of those that have the charge of the business, to bring it into the king's treasuries." And when the king hastily consented to his wicked proposal, Haman immediately sealed the decree with the king's ring, and hastened the transmission of it through all the provinces of the kingdom, that his agents might be ready for this work of destruction against the day appointed. The posts went immediately out, hastened by the king's commandment, that there might be no opportunity for recall or change. Thus the whole scheme was finished, ready to be perfectly carried out according to Haman's wish, and he was satisfied with the prospect of his revenge. "The king and Haman sat down to drink."

But what avails all this plotting against God? How mad and silly seem all the well-arranged plans of this scheme of wickedness when the providence and power of God are brought into the account! The secrecy of the plan is nothing. He that is higher than the highest regardeth it. A thousand secret agents may be at work, of which the wicked man knows nothing, to counteract all his wisdom, and overturn all his power. What a testimony we have of this in the book of Job. "'The wicked man travaileth with pain all his days, and the number of the years is hidden to the oppressor. A dreadful sound is in his ears; in prosperity the destroyer shall come upon him." A secret power of alarm and vengeance often arrests and overwhelms him in the very midst of his crime. An infinite power unseen is contending against him.

A very lovely young christian whom I well knew, was laid upon a sick bed for many years. She was often unprotected and alone. On one occasion, late at night, as she was lying awake on her bed, her family all asleep in their rooms around, a man was seen by her entering her door. He stopped a moment after he had gained an entrance, her little night lamp shining upon them both from the stand by her bed-side. He looked at this calm and lovely girl surveying him with perfect tranquillity. She raised her finger pointing upward, and said, "Do you know that God seeth you?" The man waited a moment but made no reply, and then turned and walked immediately out, having opened no other doors than the street door, and the door of her chamber. Thus God interposed and defended by the weakest instrument, but with the mightiest power. What an illustration it was of the forgotten presence of God. Ah, think of this great fact. Take it always in as a part of your account. If you sin, it is arrayed against you. If you are oppressed, it is established on your side.

Remember the story of Elisha, and his servant on the hill of Samaria, 2 Kings, vi. 15. The hill was encompassed by Syrian troops. "When the servant of the man of God was risen early, and gone forth, behold an host compassed the city both with horses and chariots. And his servant said unto him, Alas, my master! how shall we do? And he answered, Fear not, for they that be with us are more than they that be with them. And Elisha prayed and said, Lord, I pray thee, open his eyes that he may see. And the Lord opened the eyes of the young man; and he saw, and behold the mountain was full of horses and chariots of fire round about Elisha. And when the Syrians came down to him, Elisha prayed unto the Lord, and said, Smite this people, I pray thee, with blindness. And he smote them with blindness according to the word of Elisha." Thus secure and defended are they who put their trust in him, however powerful or numerous may be their persecutors and foes. The experience of Haman will soon illustrate the same important truth.

Third, we see the people whom Haman desired to destroy, given entirely into his hands. The king makes him an unlimited grant. "The king said unto Haman, The silver is given to thee, the people also, to do with them as it seemeth good to thee." They were to be sold or slain as Haman chose. The power was unlimited throughout all the provinces of the Persian kingdom. The authority was final and could not be recalled. The doom of this people seemed settled beyond recovery. No condition could appear more wretched. They were without protection and relief. They were without means of defense, or hope of deliverance. We might anticipate, as we read, their distress and despair. "Mordecai rent his clothes, and put on sackcloth with ashes, and went out into the midst of the city, and cried with a loud and bitter cry. And in every province, whithersoever the king's commandment came, there was great mourning among the Jews, and fasting, and weeping, and wailing; and many lay in sackcloth and ashes."

Alas, what extended sorrow among men the arbitrary wickedness of man is able to produce! Ambition deluges the earth with blood. The wicked covetousness of a few may doom myriads to misery, with no relief. And who would listen to the anguish of poor Jews? The cry of the captive can come into the ears of the Lord of Sabaoth alone. To surrounding men, the weeping bondman must be dumb. The pride of this world will not stop to hear—the business of this world will not stop to consider—the prosperity and self-indulgence of this world will not be troubled with the griefs of the absent suffering—the indifference of this world can not take the trouble to read, or think, or act, concerning them. In such a case there seems no earthly hope; and were it not for the God of heaven, whose eyes are in every place, and who careth for the stranger, and protecteth those who have none to help them, they must yield to final despair. Such was the condition of the Jews with Haman. Such were the early christians in the hands of pagan persecutors; and the martyrs of the Reformation in the grasp of popery more relentless than paganism; like sheep led forth to the slaughter. Such are the African slaves of our day and in our land, a race for whom it may often have been said, no man careth. Who has a tongue to speak for the dumb? Who has a heart to feel for the lowly and the oppressed? Who has time and power and patience to consider and relieve their sorrows? We may not be surprised, if in a land like ancient Persia, a whole nation of bondmen should be given without compunction or reserve into the hands of the oppressor, when, amidst all the intelligence and advancement of our time, blood can be shed like water in enormous battles for conquest, and the souls and bodies of millions can be sold to glut the appetite for human gain.

Fourth, we see on the side of the Jews no power to resist. The highest human power was irrevocably pledged to their oppressor. The royal authority was in his hands. The king was the supreme arbiter of the life of his subjects, and he had ordered their destruction. Even above the king there was the fixed and settled law that no purpose or commandment which was sealed with the king's ring might be changed; even the king himself could not reverse it. Thus did the officers of the same empire chide with Darius when he would have delivered Daniel: "He set his heart on Daniel to deliver him; and he labored till the going down of the sun to deliver him. Then the persecutors of Daniel assembled unto the king, and said unto the king, Know, O king, that the law of the Medes and Persians is, that no decree nor statute which the king establisheth may be changed." The majesty of the Persian law ruled above the king himself. There was here too a determined agency in execution. Haman's malice was unchangeable. There would be no relaxation in carrying out the scheme. All these facts combined, made the case of the Jews perfectly hopeless.

Every advantage is on the side of the oppressor. There was no opposing power to resist. How then shall arbitrary power be overthrown? How shall unjust and unrighteous laws thus established be set aside? How shall a helpless people be delivered from a determined and revengeful persecutor? How shall a people completely prostrate and weak hope for defense or attempt resistance? We can give no human answer to these questions. We survey the scene with despair. We see no possible method of deliverance or protection. But God has his own plans already laid and fixed. And he will bring out the result of his own appointment in due time. This we see in the history before us clearly displayed. Why can we not in faith equally embrace the truth and the hope in every similar case for ourselves? How much we need to learn in this matter of the dealings and plans of God's gracious providence, and of our own privileges in connection with it. All these lessons are designed to lead us to a practical, earnest faith in the care and promises of our gracious God, standing always firm in the assurance of his protection, and fixed in our choice of his service and favor.

Fifth, we are ready to ask, in reference to the case before us, how could any one ever present greater difficulties? But God delights in overcoming difficulties, and in causing the faith of his people to endure in the midst of all discouragements. He allows the obstacles in their path to accumulate to the utmost. And when there seems no hope of relief, and every thing appears desperate, then he interposes with some trivial incident, as it appears, and overthrows at once the whole power of the oppressor. Distressed as Mordecai was at the threatening evils which his people must encounter, his faith in God, their God, could by no means fail. He does not hesitate to tell Esther that "enlargement and deliverance would come from some other quarter." God would never forsake his people to whom he had given a covenant in all things well ordered and sure. He could never fail in the fulfillment of the promises which he had made to his servants and to their seed after them, to a thousand generations. This was a blessed exercise of faith in a dark and trying hour. And God graciously honored the faith which he imparted by fulfilling all its expectations in a manner the most complete. The method of the divine victory we must postpone for future consideration. It was wonderful indeed.

But I would have you learn some most important lessons from all this survey. If you come to serve the Lord, you must endure your part of the trials which his people meet. They who will live godly in Christ Jesus must suffer persecution in some shape, according to his will. Evil men and seducers will wax worse and worse. But who is he that can harm you, if you be followers of that which is good? Learn never to distrust a Saviour's care. He may tarry long sometimes; he may try your faith and patience; but let patience have its perfect work. He will never forsake you; honor him by believing it. Learn never to despond of his interference. Many disappointments may come, and you may appear to be shut up and left; but give no place to doubts. In his own time he will appear in your behalf, and by his own method, already arranged, he will give the victory to those who love him. ONLY BELIEVE; all things are possible to him that believeth. Learn never to fear the Lord's desertion of his own cause. His truth, his right, he will surely maintain, and open the way in which his cause shall surely triumph. His plans may be mysterious and obscure for a season; but let us honor him by unshrinking confidence that the cause which is right must always triumph. He will make the righteousness of his servants like the light, and their just dealings like the noonday. This in his own time he will show. Learn never to yield to the power of evil. Let no temptation induce you to prefer sin to affliction, or to shrink from trial, however severe, by any yielding of your conscience in its maintenance of duty, or of your fidelity in the service of your Lord. Ye have not yet resisted unto blood striving against sin. The Lord has called you to no heavy personal trials or conflicts for his truth. Be ready for any—nor doubt that if you are faithful, however powerful the wicked may appear, however feeble his people may seem to be, however hopeless may be the case of their distress, the government is still on his shoulder, and, from some quarter, enlargement and deliverance will surely come. Thus honor him, and he will delight to honor you.

XIX.

The Wicked Overthrown.

"I said in my heart, God shall judge the righteous and the wicked: for there is a time there for every purpose and for every work."—ECCLESIASTES, iv. 17.

THIS great fact of divine government we constantly forget. The person of the Deity is invisible. His ways and plans are not governed by the principles or the expectations of men. But the government is still on his shoulders, and he upholdeth all things by the word of his power. He is working in all the concerns of men, and brings out his own purposes in ways equally his own. The divine plans are always secret. They are announced only as they announce themselves. Though God has often proclaimed the great results he means to accomplish, he does this in general and comprehensive terms, and not in the details of his operations, and the methods of his accomplishment. Wicked men are therefore ready often to doubt his government. Scoffers arise who say, Where is the promise of his coming? They charge him with being slack concerning his promise, and indifferent to the affairs of earth; and therefore they refuse his commandments, and pursue their own chosen course of sin.

But the lesson we are studying in the school of divine providence gives us very different impressions from these. The history of Haman shows us how completely God controls the wicked and makes their crafty and malicious plans result in their own overthrow and ruin. The principle of the divine government is to make the ungodly the instruments of their own destruction. "They have made a pit and digged it, and fallen into the ditch which they made. His mischief shall return upon his own head," while the righteous against whom he plotted, shall escape.

How wonderfully this plan was illustrated in the case of Haman! We have seen him possessed of every element of power and prosperity, with no provocation to evil, and no obstructions in his path. We have seen the scheme which he had perfected to accomplish his design, with ample ability to carry it out, and his intended victims a helpless and defenseless race in his hands. Every thing was combined to give power to the man who opposed himself to God. There was almost a certainty that his scheme must be successful and the captive Jews destroyed.

But we come now to consider the peculiar method which God adopted for his overthrow. It is a wonderful illustration of the divine providence in its minuteness of application. It shows the great principle of our present text, that God has not only a purpose of judgment, but also a time already fixed, in which it is to be accomplished and displayed. "God shall judge the righteous and the wicked, for there is a time there for every purpose and for every work." The successive steps in this scheme of counteraction are very minute. It is a regular arrangement of mining and countermining, as in military assaults and sieges. Each successive step is taken in direct reference to the previous motion of the antagonist, and as secretly as possible from him.

First, God lays up in store for this future use Esther's unexpected relation to the king. It was a fearful trial of Mordecai's faith and Esther's piety. It seemed an unaccountable and dark proceeding. Their broken hearts both grieved in bitterness over the dispensation. But God was mercifully preparing for the evil to come. The hold which was allowed upon the affections, and the influence which was thus exercised upon the character of Ahasuerus, were very important in the train of results which was to be brought out. Every thing was to depend upon the will of Ahasuerus, and, therefore, such a control over his will was an effective step in the preparation. And when the whole issue comes out to view, we see for what purposes of mercy to mankind, and of benefit to Israel, Esther was brought to the throne. And when "the king loved Esther above all the women, and she obtained grace and favor in his sight," it was a manifest step in that providence which was to "bring the blind by a way they knew not, to make darkness light before them, and crooked things straight." Thus was "light sown for the righteous, and gladness for the upright in heart."

Second, God prepared a special obligation from the king to Mordecai. Mordecai overheard the expressions of some conspirators against the king's life, as he sat in the king's gate. "Two of the king's chamberlains, of those which kept the door, were wroth, and sought to lay hands on King Ahasuerus. And the thing was known to Mordecai, who told it unto Esther, the queen, and Esther certified the king thereof, in Mordecai's name." By thus revealing the plot, Mordecai became the preserver of the king's life, and the criminals were hanged upon a tree. But God allowed no reward to be given to Mordecai. The seed was sown, but the plant and the fruit were to be seen hereafter. Mordecai was permitted to go back and sit at the king's gate again, neglected and despised. Here was another early and secret step in this divine plan of protection for Israel. The fact was recorded in the chronicles of the king's book, and the purpose was written in the Lord's book; and there for the present it must remain, while the faith of the Lord's servant is still to be tried, and he must be quite content to believe and trust in a promising God alone.

Third, God interposed in the settling of Haman's lot. When Haman determined upon the destruction of the Jews, he collected his companions and agents in the scheme to cast lots for the choice of an appropriate time. In the first month of the year these lots were cast. And after casting his lot for one month after another, to select the one most advantageous to his purpose, his lot fell upon the last, the twelfth month of the year, and this he selected. "They cast the lot from day to day, and from month to month to the twelfth month." This was a very peculiar interposition. It gave nearly a year's delay to the executing of the plan. Much might be done in that time to counteract the plan and deliver his victims from his hands. This was a very effective step. The two mines were progressing, their agents shooting them forward without noise and in secret. Each was working to accomplish his plan suddenly and without previous violent display. Haman's mine was to blow up and destroy the Jews. The Lord's mine was to make Haman destroy himself. Thus God constantly arranges his providence " deep in unfathomable mines with never-failing skill." The great lesson for his people, is to trust in him, to hope for his appearing, and to leave their interests and welfare with quietness in his hands.

Fourth, God gave great ease and apparent prosperity to Haman's plan. The king granted his request at once, and gave him unlimited power to fulfill his purpose. He gave him back all the treasure he had promised for the grant, and bid him seal the decree with his own ring, that the purpose might not be changed. Thus Haman was enticed forward to perfect security. His success was so flattering to his own power that it led him to an immediate publication of his whole scheme. Twelve days of this first month only had passed, before the king's scribes were employed in writing the decrees, and the king's messengers in carrying them. "There was written according to all that Haman commanded, to the governors that were over every province, and to the rulers of the people of every province, according to the writing thereof, and to every people after their language." Thus the plan was proclaimed in every language and in every province. Nothing is more important in warfare than to induce an enemy to announce his purpose of action, and thus to overstep himself. Haman was perfectly confident in his foolhardiness, and thus rashly committed himself completely. His whole scheme of operation was everywhere proclaimed a whole year before it was to be executed, and abundant opportunity was furnished to its victims for escape, or for devising some method of deliverance. This was a special providence operating upon the mind of Haman himself.

Fifth, God endowed Esther with singular wisdom in arranging her scheme of argument and defense. She received a spirit of entire disinterestedness and devotion, willing even to sacrifice her own life for her people. We must regard this as a gift of God, and bestowed for the work for which she was to be employed. She had great skill in conducting her defense, and accomplished her desire without a suspicion of her intention in the man whom she opposed. First, she asks the king and Haman to a banquet. Nothing could appear more simple in itself, or more flattering to Haman. His mind was exalted into a perfect confidence of victory. There seemed to be now no difficulty in his path. When the queen thus united with the king in distinguishing him with personal honors, there could be no one to oppose. But why did not Esther announce her plan at this banquet? This was providence again. It was too soon yet. Another step was needful first. She is moved, therefore, simply to invite them again for a second occasion on the ensuing day. Between these two days, entirely separate from her influence, and without her knowledge, most important events were to occur in the line which she was pursuing. Yet so far as Esther was concerned the delay seemed very questionable. The king was then ready to hear, anxious to gratify her wish. Mordecai and her countrymen might reasonably complain at her wasting such opportunities of success. It appeared like planning only self-indulgence, rather than deliverance for her people. But we shall see the wisdom of her course, and the divine appointment therein. Haman was infatuated with vanity. "Then went Haman forth that day, joyful and with a glad heart." He was blind to any danger in his path. He gathered his friends and family in his own house to tell the story of his elevation and prosperity. He recounts to them all his wealth and power. "Yea," he says, "Esther, the queen, did let no man come in with the king unto the banquet that she had prepared, but myself, and to-morrow am I invited unto her also with the king." In the interval he prepares to vent his rage on Mordecai. He builds a gallows fifty cubits high, resolved to hang him thereon, and having accomplished his whole preparation and scheme for the destruction of his hated enemy, he lies down to rest. The night between the two banquets comes. What a different night to the several parties involved!

Haman intoxicated with ambition, envy and joy. Mordecai lying down in quiet submission and faith. Esther in prayer, meditating on the all-important events of the morrow. The king restless on his bed. But God the Lord was ruling over them all, and preparing for the thing which he had determined to bring to pass his work, his strange work.

Sixth, God awakens the slumbers of the king. "On that night the king could not sleep." This seemed a very unimportant fact, yet every thing depended on it. The king was awaked out of his sleep; it might be by some accidental noise, or by the state of his own excited nerves. "Uneasy lies the head that wears a crown." But what of all this? The king had awaked a thousand times before. Nothing perhaps had appeared to depend upon it then. But how important was his waking hour now! This was the last night on earth for Mordecai, according to what seemed the necessity of the case. His gallows was already erected, waiting for its victim. Haman was waiting, restless, perhaps, also, for the morning, to obtain a sure permission to hang him thereon. Every thing was arranged in a fixed succession, when the one fact on which the whole proved contingent took place. Something waked the king out of his sleep. What trifling incidents does God employ to accomplish his great results! You will sometimes hear of his providence as if it were only concerned in what men call great events; but there are no distinctions of great and little in human events before God. The most important results are often dependent on the minutest occurrences, and little facts are made great by the importance of their connections. Never be deluded by any false schemes of men. Not a sparrow falleth to the ground without the notice of your heavenly Father, and the very hairs of your head are all numbered. Try to see the hand, and to acknowledge the presence and the will of God in every thing concerning you. "In all thy ways acknowledge him, and he will direct thy paths."

Seventh, God remarkably employs the waking king. "The king could not sleep, and he commanded to bring the book of records of the chronicles; and they were read before the king."

This was a singular step. He might as readily have called for any other book. But it was a very peculiar thing, that a self-indulgent king should call for any book at all. Much more likely would it be that he should awaken his attendants for mirth and music, or for some exercise of his rage and temper, than to read to him in his sleepless hours. But thus the Lord was working in his mind to counteract the wicked Haman. The book was brought and opened at the record of Mordecai's forgotten preservation of the king, and there his attendants read. They might as naturally have read on any other page. But every thing depended on each of these separate points. All must happen as the Lord had before appointed. This was providence. Thus the Lord was shooting forward his secret mine. He is already fully under Haman's perfected scheme of ruin for Mordecai. The king demanded, "What honor and dignity hath been done to Mordecai for this?" Then said the king's servants that ministered unto him, "There is nothing done for him." Thus the sleepless night was consumed. How little did

Mordecai or Esther or Haman imagine what the Lord was himself doing, so deeply involving them all! But thus the way was prepared in which Mordecai was to be made ready for the work which he had to accomplish, and Haman was to perish in his own devices. A train of immense results for the people of Israel, reaching to future ages, was to come from this one sleepless night and this strange casual reading of the King of Persia.

Eighth, God furnished the very agent desired for the accomplishment of his plan. The early morning came, and with it Haman anxious to finish his plan for Mordecai's destruction. As the last answer was given to the king, that nothing had been done for Mordecai, Haman was heard coming "into the outward court of the king's house, to speak unto the king to hang Mordecai on the gallows he had prepared for him." Mordecai has had no reward, and Haman is to be the instrument of rewarding him. The king asks who is waiting in the court at this early hour. "And the king's servants said unto him, Behold Haman standeth in the court.

And the king said, Let him come in." Every step appears to be propitious to Haman. He enters instantly, perfectly secure of a triumphant attainment of his purpose. But God had now perfectly prepared the way for Mordecai's exaltation, and Haman, who had planned his death, must be the instrument of his honor. Let us hear the simple but inimitable account of the result in the sacred story. "Haman came in. And the king said unto him, What shall be done unto the man whom the king delighteth to honor? Now Haman thought in his heart, to whom would the king delight to do honor more than to myself?" Full of the most inordinate vanity and arrogance, Haman for a time forgot Mordecai and the gallows he had prepared. He had already the utmost exaltation for a subject. But he longed to be exhibited to the people in the royal robes and in royal state. This would seem even higher glory than a banquet with the queen. "And Haman answered the king, For the man whom the king delighteth to honor, let the royal apparel be brought, which the king useth to wear, and the horse that the king rideth upon, and the crown royal which is set upon his head; and let this apparel and horse be delivered to the hand of one of the king's most noble princes, that they may array the man withal whom the king delighteth to honor, and bring him on horseback through the street of the city, and proclaim before him, Thus shall it be done to the man whom the king delighteth to honor." Never, perhaps, was human vanity and the poor joy which comes from its gratification raised to a higher pitch. Haman's whole heart quivers with the anticipation of the king's reply. But what a reply it is to be! Before he is prepared to touch the fire to his own mine, the counter-mine beneath him is exploded. "The king said to Haman, Make haste, and take the apparel and the horse, as thou hast said, and do even so——to Mordecai the Jew that sitteth at the king's gate. Let nothing fail of all that thou hast spoken." To Mordecai the Jew! Is it possible? To Mordecai the Jew that sitteth at the king's gate! Was there ever such an overthrow before? So sudden, and so entire! Yet there can be no resistance. And Haman "took the apparel and the horse, and arrayed Mordecai, and brought him on horseback through the street of the city, and proclaimed before him, Thus shall it be done unto the man whom the king delighteth to honor."

The result is equally amazing to Haman and to Mordecai. "God shall judge the righteous and the wicked, for there is a time there for every purpose and for every work." Mordecai is to be lifted out of the dust to an exaltation divinely ordered, and Haman must be the agent in doing it. This is providence, and this was its course thus far. Every step is natural, voluntary, trifling in itself. No single step had any apparent earthly connection with the others, in the mind of the one who took it. The threads all seemed perfectly separate and unconnected. But it was a single hand which wove them all. Nothing was more likely, and nothing could seem more unimportant than each event as it occurred. But see them all together. How perfect is the scheme! How indispensable is every part! How clear the wisdom which has ordered the whole! This is the divine Providence, "the wheel in the middle of the wheel." The divine Providence over the children of God. "Whithersoever the Spirit went, thither did the wheels go also."

With what confidence we may rely on such a protector. The eyes of the Lord are in every place, beholding the evil and the good. His eyes are over the righteous, and his ears are open to their prayers. The one great object of our care is to be on the Lord's side, and under the Lord's protection. We are to seek him there where he is always to be found, in the Lord Jesus, our exalted Saviour. In him reconciled to God, we have perfect security and perfect peace, certain defense and sure prosperity. The Lord himself becomes a wall of fire round about us, and the glory in the midst of us. Jesus is himself the door of peace and hope and safety to us. Through him we may go in and out in complete assurance, and find pasture and protection according to our need. His never-failing care is over us, and however wicked men may plan, and however triumphant and powerful they may appear, we shall see our gracious Preserver ordering all, restraining all, and compelling all to promote our happiness, to enlarge our hopes, and to give us abiding and everlasting peace. Why then should we ever doubt or distrust his care? Why should we encourage a single unbelieving feeling, or ask a single anxious question. Let us trust ourselves to him in well doing, as to a faithful Creator and Redeemer. And we shall find, as Mordecai found, that there is a divine eye over us which never slumbers, and a divine power which can not be resisted or overthrown.

XX.

Unexpected Results.

"I returned and saw under the sun, that the race is not to the swift, nor the battle to the strong; but time and chance happeneth to them all."—ECCLESIASTES, ix. 11.

THE ideas of time and chance here, are simply the aspects of results as they successively appear. They are the manifestations of a secret power that is at work in addition to all that man can do, and above all the wisdom of his planning to accomplish purposes which he had not expected. They seem to him like a common chance for all. But while these are the manifestations, there is a reality of power which controls them, which decides the time before appointed for every occurrence, and allows no chance in the bringing out the result, but worketh all things after the counsel of its own will. This is the providence which we have been studying, and which we have seen so remarkably exemplified in the history of Esther.

Man's calculation is always upon the result of his own forethought and skill. There is to be a sure success from the wisdom of his plans. The race is for the swift and the battle is for the strong. Napoleon said, "Heaven is always on the side of the heaviest artillery." The history of human contests would give innumerable illustrations of the contrary. The finest calculations are disappointed, and the wisest skill proves inadequate. God vindicates his own right to rule by employing the weak things of the world to confound the mighty, and taking the wise in their own craftiness.

Haman has illustrated this in a very clear and remarkable manner. He boasted of the scheme he had laid, and the power which he possessed to accomplish it. Every step was prepared in his process with the utmost apparent certainty of the result. But he found another power at work of which he was ignorant, against which he could make no calculation and no resistance. The God of Israel was ruling in all the affairs in which he was involved, and ruling over them to produce a result entirely opposite to the scheme which he had formed.

We have traced the method of this process of man, and this process of God; the succession of steps in the mining and countermining, until the result was attained in the final and unexpected explosion. Haman listened to the king's words in perfect confidence, until he came to the one word, "Mordecai the Jew." Up to that moment every step was propitious, and every prospect was sure. Then the whole scheme exploded. All his hopes were overthrown in a moment, and the darkest apprehensions took their place. The procession which the king had ordered passed away, and Mordecai returned unmoved and unaltered to his former place, "but Haman hasted to his house mourning, and having his head covered." How different was his entrance to his house from his departure a few hours before. He went out, after a boastful preparation, to fulfill the suggestions of Zeresh his wife in hanging Mordecai upon the gallows he had made. He now returned to tell her and his friends of the sad reverse he had gone through. Little comfort or encouragement did he get from them. "Then said his wise men and Zeresh his wife unto him, If Mordecai be of the seed of the Jews, before whom thou hast begun to fall, thou shalt not prevail against him, but shalt surely fall before him." Thus faithless is a selfish world in the days of our calamity. Its friendship is enmity with God, and he that will be the friend of the world, will find himself the enemy of God.

But Haman's course is not yet complete. The lesson in this chamber of instruction does not end here, and we must trace it to its wretched conclusion, and see how God will vindicate his judgment and his truth. While Haman was conferring with his friends, the king's chamberlains came, and hastened to bring him to the banquet that Esther had prepared. At the second banquet, God had made all things ready for the complete overthrow of the ungodly, and each of the three persons assembled appeared with feelings and expectations entirely different from their state the day before. Now, Esther announced her danger and her request. " Let my life be given me at my petition, and my people at my request. For we are sold to be destroyed, to be slain and to perish." And when the astonished king demanded, "Who is he, and where is he, that durst presume in his heart to do this?" Esther could now reply with confidence and boldness, " The adversary and enemy is this wicked Haman."

Now Haman sees and feels the folly of his malice, however well contrived. He illustrates the ever-remarkable fact, that the boldest oppressor of others is the most cowardly suppliant in a returning danger upon himself. The king arose from the banquet in great wrath, and walked out into the garden of the palace. Miserable Haman arose to plead for his life before the noble woman whom he had doomed to death. How many thousands of such instancesof baseness has the world seen! Thus the infamous Jeffries cried for mercy and protection from the multitude whose sorrows he had derided, and whose relatives in multitudes he had put to death. When the king returned, Haman had fallen, in the anguish of his fear, across the very couch on which the queen reclined. An attendant, who had known the plans of Haman, said to the king, "Behold the gallows, fifty cubits high, which Haman had made for Mordecai, who had spoken good for the king, standeth in the house of Haman." Then said the king, " Hang him thereon. So they hanged Haman on the gallows that he had prepared for Mordecai. Then was the king's wrath pacified."

This closed this career of wickedness. Thus its folly and madness, as well as its guilt and certain ruin, were displayed. " Who hath hardened himself against the Lord, and hath prospered?" " I have seen the wicked in great power, and spreading himself like a green bay tree; yet he passed away, and, lo, he was not. Yea, I sought him, but he could not be found." Haman's story is an illustration of that providence which ten thousand other similar instances in the history of the world would exhibit in a like way. The scenes and the degrees may vary much; but the one great principle will always remain, and always be demonstrated in the result. The prosperity of the wicked is short; the triumph of the ungodly is but for a moment. We see it thus displayed. Why shall we ever be tempted to test it for ourselves? As the emptiness of the world displayed admonishes us not to make our portion there, and the security of true piety demonstrated encourages us to have our fellowship with those who love God, so let this exhibition of the divine providence in the punishing of the wicked, warn us not to walk in the way with them, to refrain our feet from their path, but to avoid it, to turn from it, and pass away.

And now, stand for a moment before we leave this third chamber of divine teaching, and survey the whole course of this providence as it has passed.

First, it was a train of very trifling circumstances in each particular. There has been no event in the whole succession in itself of a remarkable or unusual character. Every fact was perfectly natural to each individual concerned, to whom they severally belonged. Each person was moving naturally and independently in his own way. No one had reason to imagine that his particular course was especially dependent upon the others. Haman plotted his wickedness to gratify the malice of his own heart. Mordecai patiently endured the will of God, whom he loved and served. Ahasuerus knew no connection between Mordecai and Haman when he ordered the conclusion of his sleepless night to be carried out. Haman did not suspect the relation of Esther to the hated Mordecai and the Jews whom he sought to destroy. Esther knew nothing of the king's reading or determination, or of Haman's preparation of the gallows for Mordecai. Each of them went on in the way of his own heart and the sight of his own eyes, following and trying to accomplish his own individual plan and wish. But yet we see how remarkably a superintending divine power was controlling and directing all. There was still a wheel in the middle of the wheel. The eagle eye was watching. The calculating reason was observing and preparing. The patient steadiness was pressing calmly on. The majestic power was confident of ruling all at the proper time to the results designed. This was providence. And thus the whole manifestation of skill and wisdom and purpose, ordering the ways of each particular agent, while leaving all to act with perfect freedom, was brought out at last in a perfect exhibition.

Second, it was a very circuitous and remote process. The first step we have seen was very far off from the final result, and could not have been imagined to have any connection with it. Every succeeding step seemed equally independent and unlikely to produce the end designed. I have called it mining and countermining. The whole process was secret from all observers, and each particular process was concealed from the observation of the agents of the other. A wonderful plan was lately proposed for connecting New York and Brooklyn by a bridge, the foundation of which should be in the Park. Who that saw men digging and laying stone in the middle of the Park, with no knowledge of the plan proposed, could have imagined that it was the starting of a bridge over water so far distant, and to a shore so entirely out of sight? Yet such has been the course of this

UNEXPECTED RESULTS. 363

providence which we have considered. Stop at any point, and the connection is just as hidden, and the calculation of the future remains just as difficult. "Known only unto God are all his works from the beginning." We may stand and ask, Why should the king have selected Esther at the very time of Haman's elevation? Why should the king have awaked on the night of the very day when Haman had built his gallows? Why should Haman come into the court of the king at the very moment when the story of Mordecai had just been read? Why should Haman be called to say what ought to have been done for Mordecai? Every step is independent, unconnected apparently, and circuitous. Yet every step is sure and leading forward to the result designed. Nothing is lost, and no error is committed upon the road. This is the wonderful skill of divine Providence. The wheels are full of eyes on every side. Beneath the wings of the living creatures are the hands of a man. The utmost discernment and dexterity are displayed. And however remote appear the separate facts, they are all manifestly parts of one great plan which God has formed, and which he will surely execute.

Third, it was a perfectly unexpected result. Haman had gone through his whole preliminary course with entire success. Not an obstacle had appeared in his way. All that he had desired, and more than he had desired of the king, had been fully granted. His plan was arranged with the wisest precaution and the most entire skill. His enemies appeared to be entirely in his hands. On the last day of his career every thing around him appeared combined to facilitate and secure his triumph. His highest exaltation had been obtained when he banqueted alone with the king and queen. No previous day had been so bright as this, and he went home from it with a glad and joyful heart. He had but one more request to make, and any thing that he should ask, he was perfectly sure to obtain. He congratulated himself on the certainty of the result. To-morrow Mordecai will be slain and this one hated obstruction be removed out of his way. Thus he anticipated the issue of his course, and with entire reason, as every man observing would have said. But how suddenly and wonderfully was he disappointed. This was the very day which the Lord had prepared, the crisis of the dispensation. And he found himself required, instead of hanging Mordecai on a tree, to be the agent of his entire triumph and glorious exaltation. Yet as we have traced this course, unexpected as was its result, the process was perfectly natural. Thus we see the providence of God displayed. Why should we ever distrust or doubt its care? Let us dwell in our appointed place, and be doing good according to our Father's will, and verily we shall be protected and fed. He will make our righteousness like the light, and our just dealing as the noonday. The Psalmist says, "I have been young, and now I am old, yet saw I never the righteous forsaken, nor his seed begging their bread." The whole course of teaching through which you have been led, should lead you to confide yourselves to your gracious Saviour without a fear, exercising yourselves only to maintain before him a conscience void of offense both towards God and towards men.

Fourth, God overturned this whole scheme of wickedness without appearing directly to interfere with it in any step of the proceeding. The whole plan wrought out its own result as naturally as the seed of spring brings forth the summer's plant and the autumn's fruit. The sinner was entrapped in his own devices. As we survey the plan accomplished, every step appears to us connected and perfectly plain. But let us not forget that as it went forward every succeeding step was entirely concealed from view when the previous one was taken. The wicked man was clothed with immense power and amazing success. The sinner was deluded, by his prosperity, to suppose the race was for the swift and the battle to the strong. And yet the whole scheme was overturned in a moment, without one violent interruption occurring in its process. This is a most important lesson to us. It must teach us never to doubt the constant presence of God in all our concerns, and his directing power over all events involved in them. However threatening our disasters may appear, however immediate and certain may seem the ruin we fear, the power ruling the whole process must still control. A change of wind may turn the dreaded flame from our habitation, a sudden lull may break the force of the tempest, the very means of apparent death may be made the real instrument of security and protection. And all this may be with no remarkable interference of special divine power. The house of a friend of mine was blown down by a tempest at midnight. In the portion which was in entire ruin was his library, in which his little son was sleeping. They removed the rubbish of the ruins with dread amounting to despair. There seemed no possibility of the continuance of life to the child. But they found the little one in his night-clothes safe under a heavy library table where he had been thrown in the overturning of his little bed, and covered with loads of brick and rubbish. How many hundreds of such facts might be gathered from the experience of the people of God, showing that protecting care which is over them, and all belonging to them, guarding them in security in the midst of the utmost danger and fear. Thus should we be led to grateful trust, to affectionate prayer, and to an humble but sure expectation of the presence and power of our Lord upon our side in every crisis of danger and alarm.

Thus remarkable in the simplicity of its arrangement, as well as in the perfection of its result, was this whole process of the divine overthrow of the crafty wickedness of Haman. But when we consider the result itself, the instruction is no less important. God thus showed his divine power in this complete and easy destruction of the plot of the wicked.

He was caught in the very pride of his power. Never could the experiment be more fairly tried. The sinner had every thing on his side. Every instrument and means of success was in his hands. There seemed no opposing earthly power to resist him. Yet at the very moment of his final triumph, he was suddenly cast down. Nothing was done ostensibly to thwart his plans. So far as he could see he had no opposer and no impediment. And yet in the very last and highest point of his attainment his overthrow and destruction were complete. Ah, my young friends, learn to have faith in the promises and the power of God. The word he hath spoken must be fulfilled. His enemies may seem to have great power. Human wickedness may appear to rule without resistance or fear. And yet its overthrow must come, and the truth of God must conquer and prevail. He hath exalted his Son with his own right hand to give him the heathen for his inheritance, and the uttermost parts of the earth for his possession. He must reign till he hath put all enemies under his feet. He shall rule them with a rod of iron, and break them in pieces like a potter's vessel. And our privilege and duty is calmly to confide in his word, obey his commands and abide his will.

Haman was made the instrument of exalting the very adversary he so much hated. He came to the king at the very moment in which his mind was considering what honor should be given to Mordecai to reward him for his fidelity. He was made himself to describe the exaltation he ought to receive and himself appointed to carry it out. It was a very remarkable instance of this especial rule of providence in its details.

But it was an illustration of an habitual rule in the principles which governed it. Multitudes of similar facts distinguish the history of mankind. Many a one have I seen precisely analogous, in which the very agency of the persecution was made the instrument of success, and while the persecutor was foiled and destroyed, his intended victim was made triumphant and secure by the very preparation for his ruin. Human malice is thus made constantly to overact itself. And the things which it designs for the suffering of the children of God, he makes to promote their prosperity.

The very sorrow which he had prepared for his victim, he was himself required to endure. He had built the gallows for Mordecai, and on that very gallows he was himself hanged. There is a wonderful particularity in this system of divine punishment for men—demanding "an eye for an eye, and a tooth for a tooth," in the retributions he inflicts. Filial ingratitude habitually reproduces itself. Fraudulent increase lays up the provision for its own poverty similarly produced. Dr. Mason of New York, describes a remarkable scene of which he was an unexpected witness. A butcher in this city, in his rage with his aged father who had offended him, knocked him down upon the floor, and was dragging him by his hair to throw him into the street. He had pulled him to the outer door, when the old man cried out, " There, stop now, I did not drag him any further," and then confessed that he had abused his own father in the same manner, and dragged him to that very spot, with the same design. Such instances, in some shape, are constantly occurring, so that it is a familiar expectation, that the wicked shall fall into the pit they have digged for others, and they who take the sword perish by the sword. And we may adopt the principle thus demonstrated in providence, as a solemn warning against the indulgence of any feeling or act of malice or injustice. " Be sure your sin will find you out." " Woe to him that coveteth an evil covetousness to his house, that he may set his nest on high; for the stone shall cry out of the wall, and the beam out of the timber shall answer it." " Shall they not rise up suddenly that shall bite thee, and awake that shall vex thee, and thou shalt be for booties unto them?" No man can afford to trust himself to the secrecy of his sin, or to the prosperity of his injustice. "The Lord seeth, and the Most High regardeth; and there is a God that judgeth in the earth."

The result of this whole providence was complete deliverance and exaltation to the oppressed, and complete destruction to the oppressor. This was the final result, and an illustration of that which will always be, and at last surely be, the final result. God will exalt those whom man oppresses. They who come out of great tribulations, are seen at last with their garments washed and made white in the blood of the Lamb, and the glorious Lamb dwelling in the midst of them as their Saviour and King, leading them to living fountains of water, and crowning them with joy unspeakable and full of glory. Let the knowledge of this glorious result lead us to serve him with sincere devotion, faithful unto death, ever trusting and ever rejoicing in him alone.

XXI.

Tried Fidelity.

"The path of the just is as the shining light, that shineth more and more unto the perfect day."—PROVERBS, iv. 18.

THIS divine testimony opens for us the subject of our fourth lesson in the great school of providence in the world. It is fidelity in duty rewarded with acceptance and usefulness. It is a most precious and important principle in the divine government, one which concerns every class of men, and each individual in every class. There is no man who liveth for himself. Absolute and designated duty is imposed upon every one, lowly or exalted as he may be in earthly condition, and the fulfillment of this personal duty is that, and all that which is required of man. He may have received ten talents or one. The amount of his trust can not affect the principle of his obligation, or the motive of his services. He that is faithful in that which is least, is faithful also in much, and he that is unjust in the least, is unjust also in much. There can be no higher or brighter example given to men, than that which is found in the faithful discharge of personal duty. There can be no more valuable or attractive character than adorns those who "by patient continuance in well-doing seek for glory, honor and immortality." To them the Spirit says, "God will render eternal life."

This is the fourth lesson in the book of Esther. We have meditated in the chambers of earthly indulgence, of true piety, of malicious wickedness, and studied the lessons which are to be gathered from the views which they present; and now we pass into the chamber of active virtue to contemplate the plans of divine providence in connection with the experience and training which it receives. Here we have the fact demonstrated in a striking illustration that no man can serve God for nought. He will never be a debtor to any of his creatures. He abundantly rewards all those who do his will; and while in overturning the triumphs of the earth, he makes the first last, in the exalting and protection of his faithful servants he as surely also makes the last first. The path of truth and goodness, of love to God and love to men will always advance in light and purity to a perfect day. He that hath clean hands shall wax stronger and stronger, and though his beginning be small and feeble, his latter end shall greatly increase.

This is the illustration we have in the character and history of Mordecai. Ahasuerus, Esther, Haman, and Mordecai, in their relations make a perfect dramatic exhibition. Their paths cross each other, and their interests mingle. Their conditions and responsibilities are in constant close connection, and are continually intermingled. And yet their characters are perfectly distinct, and they act out their own principles and purposes in lines of conduct entirely separate. It is this beautifully dramatic character of the book which gives it such special interest, and renders all its facts so truly living and practical. Each character is a separate living principle. And in each the operation and result of this peculiar principle is distinctly and very beautifully displayed.

In this chamber of fidelity in duty, we first see this path of duty beginning in the very lowest circumstances of life. This is another repetition of that fact which we have already observed as a constant principle of government in the providence of God. All the advantages of position and circumstances are given to the side opposed to God. All the difficulties in the accomplishment of the divine purpose and plan are allowed, and are actually gathered in opposition. Enrich and exalt the indulgence of the world by every imagination of its wealth and pleasure, and yet he shows its end to be vanity and vexation of spirit. Depress true piety as low as sorrow, poverty and loneliness may do it, and yet he exalts it to honor and influence, and by the means of the very instruments which threatened its destruction. Arm malicious wickedness with every conceivable instrument and weapon of power and craft, and yet he takes it in its own craftiness and overthrows it in the very pride of its power. So he also illustrates the history of his purpose in the fourth manifestation of his providence which we have now to consider. He will show the reward of fidelity in duty. He will display the history of its certain triumph, and perfect security and success. Begin as low as you will in human condition. Make the sphere as limited as you can. Multiply difficulties around its strait and narrow path as you choose, and he will show you how easily and how certainly he can exalt and honor it, and that by the very instruments which have been collected to oppose it. Let the light of the just and faithful man be as little and as concealed as you may desire for your experiment and he will show you how it shall be made to shine more and more unto the perfect day.

Thus Mordecai begins a poor captive Jew, perhaps a beggar, certainly a menial at the king's gate, in the midst of a multitude crowding a royal city, and thronging the courts and entrance of the palace of the greatest monarch on earth, who neglected and despised him. "Now in Shushan, the palace, there was a certain Jew, whose name was Mordecai, the son of Jair, the son of Shimei, the son of Kish, a Benjamite, who had been carried away from Jerusalem with the captivity which had been carried away with Jeconiah, king of Judah, whom Nebuchadnezzar, the king of Babylon, had carried away." His was a poor condition, a narrow and limited sphere indeed! Men often think it of little consequence what one does who is so concealed and so little known. The duties and virtues of a beggar will be but little regarded in man's record, and rarely trumpeted by human fame. But, ah, my dear young friends, never forget that there is no such distinction before God between duties great and little, or sins venial or mortal. Whatever God requires or forbids is great. Every station which his providence has assigned and ordered is necessary and important. There is no respect of persons, no low or high with him. He regards the effort and the obedience of the beggar with as much approbation as the majesty and ruling of the prince, and the patience and prayer of Lazarus are as precious in his sight as the bounty and benevolence of the rich man at whose gate he lies.

Virtue must always be tried by little things. The beginnings of all temptations are small, and the question of resistance or compliance with them is always settled in very narrow contingencies of trial. It is far easier to perform higher duties, and to resist greater temptations. The real trial of human principles is in unknown and secret dangers. The more secret and apparently uninfluential is a habit of sin, the more dangerous, and the more to be dreaded it becomes. When everybody is watching, it is easy to walk uprightly. The soldier on parade will be sure to keep time and step. But when our walk is unobserved, our conduct unnoticed, our position in life of no consequence in human sight, then are our difficulties and our temptations always the greater and the more dangerous. If Mordecai should sin or fail in duty, in his dark and narrow circle, who will know it? How many argue thus. It is for this reason that the illustration is presented to us, in the narrowest sphere of life. We feel the temptation often and strongly in similar condition. The wandering eye, the lustful desire, the impure imagination, even the positive allowance and indulgence—how often are they permitted and obeyed, because we are in a place of strangers, or hidden from view, or out of reach by those whose judgments we might dread! No one will know; no one sees; example is nothing; it is of no consequence what I do; it is impossible for me to do much good in any way. Ah, not thus did Mordecai argue, though in these very circumstances of narrow influence Mordecai begins.

Second, we see this poor and faithful man perfectly contented with his low estate. He is unmurmuring though poor. Of his early condition in the story, we only know that he was a Jewish captive in Persia, a worshiper of the true God in a heathen land, and exposed to all the trials which followed that people in those peculiar circumstances. Here we know but little of his domestic circumstances. Happy and quiet in his lowly home, probably none was there beside, save this lonely orphan child whom he had adopted as his own, for when she was taken from him he made his abode at the king's gate. His affections and anxieties were devoted to her. Yet thus is he brought before us, with no complaint that his sphere is not sufficiently large, or that his comforts are restricted and few. He frets not against the appointment which has placed him in his low condition. Patiently and simply he fulfills his present work, believes in the promises of his covenant God, and waits in his narrow line of duty for the Lord's direction and appointment.

I beg you to contemplate such a description. How valuable and desirable is such a spirit! How precious to all his servants is that blessed testimony of the Lord, "He that is faithful in that which is least, is faithful also in much." Go, fulfill well your appointed work. Stop not to discuss its comparative advantages or difficulties. Receive it, whatever it may be, as a special divine commission for yourself, a part in the great family of God, which he sees particularly adapted to you, and which he has therefore selected and appointed for you. It is the very state and condition in which you are most qualified to glorify and honor him. If you would have larger and higher responsibility, gain it and be prepared for it, by earnestly and contentedly fulfilling the obligations which are laid upon you now. This is virtue, obedience to God, and this alone. Multitudes forfeit all their prospects by neglecting their present obligations, by claiming to judge and decide on the seat of government, rather than being contented to submit and obey as creatures and servants who are dependent. Abide with thankfulness in the calling wherein you are called, and dignify it by a holy walk, tranquilize it by a spiritual mind, and adorn it by a conversation becoming the gospel, which is the great and unspeakable gift of God and makes all other gifts precious and happy. This is the attractive aspect of the illustration which is before us here.

Third, we see him affectionate and liberal in his social relations. Though poor, yet making others rich. Pitiful and courteous, affectionate and tender; these are indispensable qualities of that virtue which is acceptable to God. He who deeply feels his obligations to God, will also feel a love for all whom God also loves, especially for those whom God has been pleased to make in any way dependent on his own kindness and love. Tenderness in domestic relations, kind and conciliatory feelings and deportment, forbearance with annoying circumstances, and an earnest effort to multiply the joys of others, are lovely fruits of piety, of youthful piety in particular. They not only prompt to acts of usefulness and love, but they minister them in a way which doubles their value, and clothes them with peculiar power and influence in the example they present. This aspect of character shines in special display in the case before us. Though poor himself, he cheerfully adopts his orphan cousin, and divides his comforts, whatever they might be, with her. " He brought up Hadassah, his uncle's daughter." The orphan child was left in a forsaken infancy. " She had neither father nor mother; whom Mordecai took, when her father and mother were dead." This was true liberality devising liberal things. True liberality is in the spirit which prompts the act, not in the amount of the act itself. The poor widow who threw her two mites into the treasury, cast in more than all beside. The largest generosity is often among the most straitened in earthly condition. But it is an indispensable characteristic of true virtue. Obedience to God is imitation of God, who giveth liberally and upbraideth not. Nor can any thing with justice be called human excellence which is destitute of this noble spirit. A covetous, harsh, narrow, selfish temper can never have tasted that God is gracious, or have known any thing of the Saviour's transforming love. This attribute of excellence Mordecai illustrated.

He was delicate and refined in his liberality. There is much in the way in which kindness is bestowed to make it either acceptable or a burden. The little orphan, Mordecai "took and brought up for his own daughter." No description could have given a picture of his character in this relation, more tender, or pure, or beautiful. This refinement is always an attribute of true excellence, and to be cultivated and valued as such exceedingly. There is nothing in the religion of the New Testament to encourage bluntness, coarseness or assumption of superiority. Love, acting in beneficent effort, expressing itself in patience, humility, sympathy, cordial long-suffering, this is the spirit and the character which the gospel requires and gives. What a world would this be should this heavenly spirit and relation be universally and thoroughly carried out! But Mordecai's tenderness was watchful as well as delicate. When his beloved ward was taken from him by a force which he could not resist, his own house had lost all its charm for him. "To know how Esther did, and what should become of her," was the dearest interest he had on earth. And for this "he walked every day before the court of the women's house." Tidings from her was the great object of his desire, and the faithfulness of his affection was thus constant and earnest. And when Esther was finally taken to the king's house, Mordecai went and "sat in the king's gate." His whole heart and interest were there, and there henceforth, a faithful watchman over his lost child, would he abide. This attractive character of tenderness and affection runs through the whole of Mordecai's history, and is displayed in every relation. And it gives a peculiar charm to that lowly but shining virtue which he displays, and renders his life yet more exemplary on this account.

Fourth, we see him faithful in every claim as a subject. It was one of the peculiar exercises of the divine Providence which carried him at the time to sit at the king's gate. There, wrapped up in his own meditations and sorrows, his presence was not regarded by those who were officially employed. In his solitude he overheard the counsel of two conspirators against the life of the king. This king was the very one who had snatched from him the treasure of his heart, and violently taken his lovely orphan to minister to his own pleasure in the confinement of the palace. Yet Mordecai had no feeling of pleasure in listening to plans of evil against the man who had injured him. He made known to Esther the discovery he had made, and Esther, imitating his fidelity, delivered the intelligence to the king in Mordecai's name. As a captive Jew he might have rejoiced in the danger of the oppressor of his people. As a poor, despised man he might have been indifferent to the whole matter, and said, "Of what consequence is it to me? I can be no worse off than I am." But neither of these was the temper of Mordecai. He felt it the duty of a subject to guard the ruler's life, whoever he might be. He acknowledged the appointed obligation upon Israel to "seek the peace of the city whither the Lord had led them in captivity." And as the servant of God he realized the obligation to do good to all men, and especially to pray for and protect those in authority over him. He sought the opportunity, therefore, to preserve the life of the king, and he succeeded.

This also is an eminent example. The virtuous, religious man is always an orderly and peaceful man. The followers of the Lord Jesus will always be the imitators of his peace-making spirit, and reverence, as they are taught in his word, those who are in authority over them. Never was this example more important than in our day, when a strong and universal propensity to revile and rebel against authority and law is a growing characteristic. We can not too strongly reprove a habit and taste like this. One of our first duties is to pray for those who are in authority, to strengthen their hands in the discharge of appointed duty, and to sympathize with the burdens and responsibilities which stations of high authority bring. And when boldness and virulence of assault, reviling, scurrilous and abusive attacks, resistance and contempt of official rights and powers, take the place of these in public papers, and in the conversation of men, the aspect is shocking to our moral sense, and the example is ruinous to our youth. Fidelity in duty can never countenance or tolerate a temper like this. And true virtue in our social relations, though it may feel the oppression of wrong, will leave the exercise of punishment to him to whom vengeance alone belongs.

Sixth, we see in Mordecai especial fidelity to God. We can not impute his refusal of homage to Haman to any other motive than this.

Due reverence to authority it was not his disposition to refuse. But the homage to a man of such impiety, which his vanity delighted in, and upon which his pride insisted, Mordecai, as a faithful servant of God, could not consent to offer. He sat quietly in the king's gate when the enemy of his people passed. Nothing would he do or say against him. He would be a partner of no violence and no reviling. But he would not be a partaker of other men's sins. He would not prostrate himself in humiliation before any but God alone. This was a special illustration of his fidelity. Three faithful youths of his captive nation, more than a century before, had said in like fidelity to the king of Babylon, when he had threatened them with the burning fiery furnace on a similar refusal, " O Nebuchadnezzar, we are not careful to answer thee in this matter. If it be so, our God, whom we serve, is able to deliver us from the burning fiery furnace, and he will deliver us out of thy hand, O king. But if not, be it known unto thee, O king, that we will not serve thy gods, nor worship the golden image which thou hast set up." Thus Mordecai stood in the integrity of his soul towards God. It seemed to others around a little thing when they remonstrated with his refusal. But no principle of duty is a little thing to a faithful servant of God. The scale may be small; the field may be narrow; but the principles involved are just as important, and he can not sacrifice or neglect them. What an example is this! How easy and how tempting are the inducements to false compliances, and how frequent are the concessions made to sinful custom, by those who are mainly and habitually right. But let us adopt and adhere to the line of strict and simple conformity to the will of God, in every thing determined to do that which pleaseth him; exercising ourselves to maintain a conscience void of offense towards him. Thus shall we glorify him and find acceptance with him. And thus will he make even our enemies at peace with us, and bring forth our integrity and just dealing at the last, like the light, and as gold tried in the fire. Happy will be your condition, however lowly, if you walk consistently and sincerely with God. Then in peaceful hope may you trust in him; in affectionate prayer may you go to him; in conscious union and fellowship with him, may you rejoice in him; and look upward and forward to his presence, as to the Father whom you have loved, without a doubt of his acceptance, and with a sure promise of the inheritance of his glory.

XXII.

The End in Peace.

"Mark the perfect man, and behold the upright; for the end of that man is peace."—PSALM xxxvii. 37.

WHAT can be more valuable to the youthful mind than the train of instruction through which we have passed? How remarkably, in every step, the divine providence vindicates itself—manifests the equity of its own principles and proceedings, and gives certain triumph to principles of truth and habits of obedience in those whom God loves and protects.

The chamber of instruction in which we now are, has claims to universal interest. Man's relation to God, who made, preserves, redeemed, and will judge him, is his inevitable condition and characteristic. Whatever may change beside, this can never change. It depends upon no circumstances of his outward being; it lies under all possible experience of joy or sorrow, of elevation or depression in his earthly state. He is in every thing what he is toward God.

The demand of this universal relation may be expressed in the single word DUTY—man's duty to God. Was this ever more perfectly expressed than in the language of our Catechism? "My duty towards God is to believe in him, to fear him and to love him with all my heart, with all my mind, with all my soul and with all my strength; to worship him, to give him thanks, to put my whole trust in him, to call upon him, to honor his holy name and his word, and to serve him truly all the days of my life." This is the universal, unchangeable demand upon man, upon every man. Fidelity to God is that ornament in the sight of God of great price, which may adorn every condition, and honor equally the poorest and the most exalted of mankind.

The stations in human life vary immensely. The apparent importance to others of individual men varies as remarkably. But there is no difference before God. The same obligations are upon all. The same motives are given to excite and encourage all. The same promise of acceptance rewards all. And the highest and the lowest stand undistinguished by any such circumstances of their condition before God, who trieth the hearts of all, and judgeth according to the heart of each. This is a most important subject for youthful consideration. Fidelity to God is the one constant trial for man, for which the recompense is sure, and the result glorious. Success to genius, to great personal talents, is earthly, and peculiar to a few. It shines in special cases, but often with a glare entirely false and ruinously delusive. But success to faithfulness, even in the narrowest sphere and with the feeblest powers, is uniform and certain, and, as an example, blessed and wholesome. This is a prize which all may win, and which the poor and lowly may enjoy with as real and abiding certainty as the powerful and prosperous. This is the great principle which Mordecai illustrates.

In his case we first see this fidelity for a period exceedingly tried and hopeless. Mordecai had seated himself in the king's gate to console his solitude and sadness by the nearest possible approach for him to the one earthly object of his faithful affection and care. Into that palace his beloved Hadassah had been carried, and no other spot of earth had attractions to lead him away from it. But there seemed to be no hope before him. She could never return to him. There appeared no prospect of gain or security to him. A poor despised Jew, where the enemy of the Jews had absolute dominion, could have no prospect of usefulness, hardly of safety. It appeared for a moment a gracious providence that he had discovered the threatened murder of the king, and a gleam of hope glanced before him for the time. But all this passed, and Haman's hostility prepared a sad contrast to any hope for him. He was neglected and forgotten. He could not have known that even in the chronicles of the king's book any record of him or of his fidelity was made. And he sat there probably covered with his robe in sorrow, shunning observation, and shrinking from a possible discovery of his condition or his emotions. But even there Mordecai had a conscience and a heart at rest. He could wait and trust, and hope in God, however dark might be his prospect and however neglected he might seem to be. We see who was caring for him and leading him on to great and abounding blessings, however little he could see of the way in which he was to go.

But this was divine providence with him. Similar to this may be the trial of many. All things for a time may seem to be against them. It is a trial for patience. Will faith hold out? Can they be faithful to the end in their appointed course, with no eye to an earthly reward? Will they abide and persevere in doing right for the sake of right, without a recompense, or the attractions of a recompense, in any of the things of the present life? This is a great trial. But it is an opportunity for a glorious victory. There is a strong temptation to be hasty in judgment, and to adopt wrong methods for personal deliverance and relief. But true faithfulness to God waits upon God and leaves the whole arrangement of the course and the result to him. This patient, waiting heart is a blessed attainment and gift. It is the security of a final triumph, and the insurance of a present abiding peace.

Second, we see this faithfulness in duty brought to extreme danger. Not only was Mordecai unrewarded, but he was condemned to an appointed destruction. God appeared to have forgotten him, while his enemies prevailed against him. He was made the innocent cause of apparent ruin to his nation, and amidst the ruin to be brought upon them, his own death seemed to be inevitably involved. But beyond this, a personal destruction was prepared expressly for him. Haman, all-powerful, had already erected the gallows for his execution, and it seemed impossible that he should escape. And however ignorant he might have been of the personal ruin impending over him, his danger, in the common destruction of his countrymen, was perfectly apparent to him. "He rent his clothes and put on sackcloth with ashes, and went out into the midst of the city and cried with a loud and a bitter cry." The crisis was terrifying indeed, and the danger, as it appeared to him, extreme and imminent. Yet his faith held out. He still rested in the assurance that "enlargement and deliverance should arise to the Jews" from some quarter. And distressed and overwhelmed as he was, he was not deserted or in despair. Thus God is often pleased to try the faith of his servants, and to prove their fidelity in duty. They must sometimes hope even against hope, and trust themselves to God, and believe in the word of God assuring defense and protection to his people, though every fact which is seen, and every calculation which man can make, may seem to minister only objections. The one grand defense is faith in God, trust in his promise and confidence in his power. While faith holds out, difficulties are comparatively unimportant. All things must work together for good to those who love God. We see this demonstrated in Mordecai's case, in all the prosperity which he subsequently obtained. An extended observation of the providence of God would show a similar demonstration in multitudes of instances. Our privilege and duty is to rest upon his promise, to trust in his care, and to wait in perfect contentment and submission for his appointed time and way for our deliverance. The soul that is at rest in Jesus can never be forsaken. There is no condemnation for those who are in Christ Jesus, and no device or art against them can ever prosper.

Third, we see this fidelity in duty completely rescued and delivered. The danger passed as unexpectedly as it came. An unseen protector was revealed in the accomplishment of his own work of faithfulness to his servant, and showed himself to be present and careful over those who love him, however little his interposition might have been expected by their enemies. The way in which the hand of God interposed was signal and worthy of special remark. Suppose the question had been proposed in an exhibition of all the danger to which Mordecai was exposed, How shall he be delivered? What a different scheme man would have proposed. Perhaps what a variety of suggestions might have been made. But what plan could be more perfect than that which made the same hand that was to destroy the instrument of saving? We have traced this whole process in our review of all the actors therein. The ruin is averted from Israel, and the threatened death is turned away from Mordecai by a divine overruling of the mind of the king, and a selection of Haman as the very agent for Mordecai's defense and exaltation. Thus God perfects his own salvation, and carries on the work which he undertakes, by his own power alone. Who ever trusted in him and was confounded? He delivers the souls of his servants out of all their troubles, and rescues them from the hand of every enemy. What dangers may surround us we can never tell. And I doubt not, we shall be able to look back upon many which were wholly unknown to us, that would have appeared terrifying in the extreme could we have understood them as they were gathering over us. But the divine power interposed for deliverance even before we knew that any deliverance was required. We may thus always trust in God's gracious care, and leave every thing concerning us to him. Are we indeed not our own, but bought by him with a price? Then

will he not preserve and defend the body and
the spirit which are his? What is our being but
for him? Our single care is to be his, to do his
will perfectly and completely; to serve him without carefulness, and to entrust the guardianship
and the supply of all our wants completely
to him. It is impossible that any being or
thing can harm us if we are truly followers
of that which is good. Thus Mordecai proved
the success and the security of the path of duty,
and thus may we always find ourselves guarded
and preserved, while, reconciled in Jesus, we
serve him with a pure heart fervently, and make
it the single purpose of our heart to do his will.

Fourth, we see this fidelity in duty proportionably exalted. How suddenly and how unexpectedly the time and the arrangement for
the honor came! Mordecai was sitting as usual
in the king's gate, solitary and unnoticed. His
mind was probably at the very moment engaged
upon his own sorrows and dangers. The anguish of heart for his own people was intense;
and in the solitude of his meditations, their possible deliverance, and how it might be effected,

filled and occupied his mind, when suddenly a royal messenger came to summon him within the court. The natural, immediate conclusion was some new danger to be encountered. The mind used to grief is fertile in imagining new griefs to come. But Mordecai follows the messenger, and what a surprise awaits him! The royal robes are held up before him; the king's own horse caparisoned stands before him; attendants are collected, waiting for him; Haman, his enemy, meets him with reverence and honor. What can it all mean? He is clothed in gorgeous apparel, seated upon the king's own horse, and Haman, the enemy who hated and despised him, is the attendant to lead his horse, and to proclaim in triumph before him, "Thus shall it be done unto the man whom the king delighteth to honor." The whole scene, however transitory, is amazing to him—probably in its connection it was at the time wholly unintelligible. But its purpose and relation are plain to us. Fidelity in duty can not always be forgotten. The hour of its recognition and triumph will come. The faithful servant of the King of kings is the one whom that King delighteth to honor. Seasons of depression may pass over you; times of darkness and forgetfulness may cover you; you may imagine yourselves passed over and out of mind; but if you are faithful in your appointed sphere, the divine eye is always watchful, and the mind of God always observing. God will bring out his plans unexpectedly and surely. In the very midst of your darkness, light from above shall shine around you; and in the proportion of your trials and sufferings in your Master's work, shall be the honor which he will place upon you, in his own time and way. I would that I could impress this all-important thought upon you. You have but one thing on earth to do, the will of your Father in heaven. Your interests, welfare, happiness, security, are entirely in his hands, perfectly safe under his guardianship, and he can and will make the things which were planned by others for your injury, combine to promote your greater and abiding welfare. Be patient and faithful, and trust yourselves to him, in well-doing. Glorify him in your body and your spirit, which are his, and your honor and exaltation shall come in due time.

Fifth, we see this fidelity in duty abundantly rewarded in outward, earthly things. Delivered from imminent death, shining in manifested exaltation and acknowledgment, Mordecai finds himself to be prospered still further than this. The house of Haman is made the property of Mordecai. The wicked perisheth and the righteous cometh in his place. Haman's office and authority are bestowed upon Mordecai. The king's ring is transferred to him, and he is permanently exalted to be the minister of the king, and the special agent of his authority in the nation. "Mordecai went out from the presence of the king in royal apparel of blue and white, and with a great crown of gold, and with a garment of fine linen and purple; and the city of Shushan rejoiced and was glad." What a contrast of circumstances and conditions a few days have accomplished! But nothing is too hard for the Lord. This is a manifestation of the divine providence, a token and pledge of his fidelity to his people. God will leave none of his works unfinished. The result will always show how sure a paymaster he is to those who serve him; how certain they who are faithful to him may be of his fidelity to them. He may not give to all riches and honor, in outward things; but he will keep all who love him from want and suffering; he will give that contentment with godliness which makes his service a great gain; and their sure enjoyment and inheritance of all the happiness which even earth can give, will exhibit the fulfillment of his promise, and vindicate the unfailing certainty of his truth. A full investigation and intelligence of the history of his dealings with his people will always show the certain prosperity, even in earthly things, which attends obedience and fidelity to him. A small thing that the righteous hath is better than great riches of the ungodly. Their dwelling place is the tabernacle of his presence and love, and their most moderate provision under his gracious benediction is a continual feast. Thus Mordecai proves the faithfulness of the God whom he serves; and as we study the lesson which his experience and history furnish in this chamber of instruction, and see its principles and illustrations repeated in all the plans and arrangements of the divine providence in the world around us, and in the history of the Lord's family upon earth, we see how perfectly sure is the hope of all who love him, and how full and abundant the recompense which his service gives, even in the temporal and earthly results which attend it.

Sixth, we see this fidelity in duty not only rewarded in itself, and in the person and condition of the man who is distinguished by it, but crowned with eminent usefulness to others. God was pleased thus to exalt Mordecai in a very eminent degree. He was immediately commissioned to counteract all of Haman's schemes of cruelty to the people of his own nation, and to be the instrument of a great deliverance and protection to them. "Ahasuerus said unto Esther the queen, and to Mordecai the Jew, Behold, I have given Esther the house of Haman, and him they have hanged upon the gallows, because he laid his hand upon the Jews. Write ye also for the Jews as it liketh you, in the king's name, and seal it with the king's ring." This privilege Mordecai gladly and instantly embraced, and hastened his messengers through every province of the kingdom, that the deliverance might be sure, and the preparation in adequate season for all his people. Faithful before in that which was least, Mordecai was now faithful in that which was much. The same spirit of obedience which had made him patient, submissive and quiet in enduring the trials of his earlier condition, prepared him to be now active and earnest in his beneficent action for the people committed to his care, in the royal office and power now entrusted to him. Under his dominion as the royal minister, "the Jews had light, and gladness, and joy, and honor, in every province and in every city, whithersoever the king's commandment and his decree came." Thus was this faithful man exalted to rule in final and sure prosperity. Such honor have all the Lord's saints. What a blessing does a really godly man become in exalted and influential station; nay, what a blessing he may be in every station! How extensively any such one may be an instrument of divine blessing to his fellow-men, he can never tell. Thousands whom he can never see on earth, may derive encouragement and strength from his example. Ages after him may learn new consolation from the Lord's gracious dealings with him. Mordecai becomes a blessing not merely to his own generation or people, but to all the servants of God who read the story of his fidelity and success, in every land and in every age.

I need not recount minutely all the details of this direct agency of Mordecai upon his own nation. The twelfth month of the year, the month which had been designated by Haman's lot for the destruction of the Jews, arrived. "The day drew near on which the enemies of the Jews hoped to have power over them." But in this overrruling providence which we have traced, by this "wheel in the middle of a wheel," "it was turned to the contrary, that the Jews had rule over them who hated them, and no man could withstand them, for the fear of them fell upon all people; and all the rulers of the provinces, and the lieutenants, and the deputies, and the officers of the king helped the Jews, because the fear of Mordecai fell upon them. For Mordecai was great in the king's house, and his fame went throughout all the provinces; for this man Mordecai waxed greater and greater." This great deliverance was not to be forgotten. Another decree from Esther and Mordecai was issued abroad among all the Jews to make it "a day of gladness and of feasting, and a good day, and of sending portions one to another and gifts to the poor; and that these days should be remembered and kept throughout every generation, every family, every province and every city, and that these days should not fail from among the Jews, nor the memorial of them perish from their seed." Thus fidelity in duty, tried and established virtue, gained its earthly reward, under that gracious providence which allows no man to serve God for nought. And as we trace the history of its trial and its recompense in Mordecai, we can not but feel the encouragement which his example imparts, and receive instruction from the principles of divine government which the story of his experience displays. It is a lesson of the utmost value for us, and it ought to be made the instrument of abiding usefulness to us.

But we must not close our view of the history of Mordecai without remarking particularly upon the final description which is given us of his condition and character in the result of his whole probation. "For Mordecai the Jew was next unto King Ahasuerus, and great among the Jews, and accepted of the multitude of his brethren, seeking the wealth of his people, and speaking peace to all his seed." What an illustration is this, may I not say, what a type it is of the character and office of our great and gracious Redeemer! Thus the Lord Jesus stands as the appointed Ruler of the people of God. He took upon him the seed of Abraham, in the family of Jacob, and was made a lowly, suffering man. He was despised and rejected of men, though no deceit or guile was found in him. He was an outcast among men, and doomed to a death of condemnation and sorrow upon the accursed tree. He really tasted death upon the cross for every man, and because death could have no dominion over him he arose from the dead and ascended on high far above all things in heaven and in earth. There he is exalted at the right hand of God, a prince and a Saviour to give repentance to Israel and forgiveness of sins. Was there ever a description of him in this exalted and glorious work more appropriate? "Accepted of the multitude of his brethren." What millions whose nature he assumed, and of whose flesh and blood he was a partaker, have rejoiced in his salvation, and delighted to receive the mercies he so freely bestows. They stand around his throne in triumph, clothed in the garments of his salvation, and covered with the robe of his righteousness, and rejoicing to be fed and nourished by his grace for ever. They have received him in their hearts with perfect confidence and delight, and he is their everlasting triumph and joy. Millions still in their pilgrimage on earth have received him also in a grateful acceptance of his mercy, trusting wholly in his power to save, and hoping with joyful confidence in the fullness of his everlasting love. All whom the Father hath given to him shall come unto him. And whosoever cometh unto him he will in no wise cast out. "Seeking the wealth of his people and speaking peace to all his seed." Thus he ministers with unceasing mercy to the souls of his redeemed. Durable riches, an inheritance of light, a kingdom which can not be moved, he gives to each of them. He sets them upon a throne of life and they reign with him for ever. He ministers to them all everlasting peace, peace with God in the complete forgiveness of sin, and peace passing understanding ruling within their own conscience and heart, the special manifestation of his presence and power. Peace amidst all the trials of earth, peace in the hour of departure, peace eternal in the heavens. Such, and so gracious and blessed is the great Ruler of the saints of God, the Prince of Peace. Thus does he stand before you for your acceptance and love. Whosoever trusteth in him can never be confounded. Thus is he ready to impart his mercies to you all. And the study and experience of his providence should lead you to rest yourselves on him, to delight in him as your great and glorious Lord, and to make perfectly sure your everlasting portion with him.

CONCLUSION.

This is the just conclusion of our present study, and the real design of the gracious providence of God with us. His merciful providence leads us to the enjoyment of his abounding grace. Its great purpose, with all his people, is to bring them to the Saviour who hath died for them, and then to instruct, edify, and keep them still more affectionately, completely, and eternally united to him. Our study of this book of providence completes itself in a revelation of this Saviour to our view in all his fullness and power; and our experience of the actual divine providence with us, will, under the sanctifying guidance of the Holy Spirit, complete itself in our personal enjoyment of the Saviour's love and the Saviour's grace for ever.

Then with all his redeemed, we may sing that great song of Moses and the Lamb, "Great and marvelous are thy works, Lord God Almighty; just and true are thy ways, thou King of saints."

THE END.

www.ingramcontent.com/pod-product-compliance
Lightning Source LLC
Chambersburg PA
CBHW030556300426
44111CB00009B/1007